ONE ACTION NOW™

GET FOCUSED, STAY ON TRACK, AND GET MORE DONE IN YOUR BUSINESS

KARYN GREENSTREET

Passion For Business Publications
PO Box 25, Saylorsburg, PA 18353 | (610) 381-4332
www.passionforbusiness.com

Although the author and publisher have made every effort to ensure the accuracy and completeness of the information contained in this book, we assume no responsibility for errors, inaccuracies, omissions, or any inconsistency herein. Any slights of people, places, or organizations are unintentional.

First printing 2016
Second printing 2018

CONTENTS

ACKNOWLEDGMENTS

How can I thank all the people who have helped me along the way?

To my husband, Aly, whose incredible love and support has sustained me these many years – thank you for the deep conversations, encouraging words, and endless cups of coffee. Together we have created a business and a life that mirrors our true values, and sharing it all with you has been an amazing adventure.

A deep, heart-felt thank you to my parents and family, who always told me I could become anything I wanted. You taught me the value of perseverance and focus. You'll be happy to know I outgrew the messy teenager phase.

To my colleagues, clients, members, and students – many times we've talked and brainstormed together, and you gave me detailed feedback on this book. I'm so grateful for the insights and inspiration. This book was written for you.

A huge shout out to Laura Hess, Jennifer Kellogg, Diane Fraley and Charlene Burke for being advanced readers of *One Action Now*. Your insights and edits are greatly appreciated.

A special thank you to my BrainTrust mastermind group – because, after all these years together, you *know* what it takes to birth a new book.

Action is the foundational key to all success.

– PABLO PICASSO

THE STORY BEHIND THE BOOK

I've been a small business owner for all my adult life. I opened my photography studio one month after I graduated from college, and plunged headlong into the entrepreneurial world.

It didn't start well. I was the world's biggest procrastinator and the sloppiest, most disorganized person you could ever meet. How can those traits yield a successful business?

Naturally, I struggled. Too often details got misplaced, projects were in a tangle, and tight deadlines meant burning the midnight oil. Weddings are a one-time event: the expectation of the day being "perfect" are everywhere. I can remember late nights with my team, assembling wedding albums around the kitchen table because the bride was arriving the next day to pick it up. Some weekends I was shooting three weddings, then rushing around the following week to quickly create and sort the proofs before the bride and groom returned from their honeymoon. There were a million other tasks, all vying for my attention - fielding phone calls from prospective clients, handling invoicing, paying bills, ordering supplies, designing marketing campaigns – the list was endless.

I squeaked by with a lot of luck – and to the outside world I appeared successful. But I didn't feel that way inside. Instead of being happy and proud, I felt frazzled.

I realized that my typical working style wasn't sustainable. And if I wanted to *grow* the business, it was laughable to think I could do it with my normal chaos and clutter.

Over several years I taught myself how to manage my time, projects, and energy so I could run an efficient and successful business. I changed my habits and my mindset, and my business flourished.

Many years later, I became a small business consultant. I saw a mirror of my early experience in the lives of my clients. They were all struggling to manage their projects and juggle priorities with limited time and resources. They repeatedly said, "I'm overwhelmed. I don't know what to work on first when everything needs my attention." So, I showed them the tricks and techniques I had learned the hard way, and watched their businesses bloom as they shifted from pandemonium to planning.

I began teaching my One Action Now system in 2010 to other small business owners. I watched my students organize their goals and tasks, and finally finish important projects.

In the past 30 years, I've owned five businesses and sold three of them. I've worked with thousands of small business owners, and together we solved their action planning and time management dilemmas – and in this book, I share with you their success stories and my complete One Action Now system.

Once you understand it and put it into daily practice in your own business, you'll be happier and more productive...and more profitable, too.

Always forward, ever upward,

Karyn

KARYN GREENSTREET
Founder, The Success Alliance and Passion For Business, LLC

WHAT SHOULD I WORK ON NEXT?

As a small business owner, you struggle to find the answers to questions like these:

- What's the next *right* project to initiate?
- What's the next most *important* task to finish?
- How do I juggle my time so I can grow my business and run it efficiently?

The answer is simple:

Choose the one action to take right now which will have the greatest impact and move you towards your goals. *Pick one action now and do it.*

However, it's daunting and challenging to select which of your goals are most important. Add to that the stress of figuring out how your goals fit into the big picture of your business, and then choosing one action to take.

Follow along as I walk you through my One Action Now system, a step by step process for making wise decisions and getting into action without feeling overwhelmed. When you have a smart action plan, everything is possible in your business.

Why Is It Called One Action Now?

One Action Now is based on an ancient part of your brain – and how you can overcome your built-in biology and chemistry. A part of your brain called the amygdala can rule your life and habit. The job of the amygdala brain is to keep you safe.

The amygdala sleeps most of the time, but any large change, any possible threat or stressor (like big goals and giant projects) can awaken that sleeping amygdala, which triggers the flight or fight response. It's functioning exactly the way it was designed to function.

I designed One Action Now to keep your amygdala happy and safe. Happy Amygdala equals Happy Project Implementation. See? It's easy if you know the tricks!

What Happens When You Attempt Project Planning

The amygdala can't tell a real threat from a perceived threat. If you're heading down a one-way street and a car is racing towards you, that triggers the amygdala.

So, does simply *thinking about and imagining* a car hurtling towards you on a one-way street.

When you *think* that a project is huge or a task is too complicated, it triggers the amygdala. You'll have the same stress reaction as when a car is racing towards you head-on.

Anytime you veer away from your normal behavior (like starting a colossal project, or working on new or uncomfortable tasks), your amygdala interprets that as a threat to your survival. This stress reaction triggers a cascade of hormones in your body – and your palms get sweaty and your heart starts to race.

This stress reaction can reduce creativity and rational thought. Your amygdala wants to harness *all* your resources for running away or fighting. This isn't ideal when you need your creativity and your logical mind to complete some of these projects and tasks.

Harness your amygdala and get focused on planning in a simple way. You'll feel less stressed and more confident, find creative solutions, make wiser decisions, and move your business in the right direction.

Set Your Focus as You Read

Let's start with a quick question: Do you have one area in your life where you want to make a change?

When I ask this question in my classes, I always hear laughter. "Just *one* area?" the participants ask.

I'm the same as you. Every year I write a massive list of goals. And I complete most of them. That's what I want for you. That's what the One Action Now system helps you achieve.

One Action Now is all about creating your plans for the next 12 months. It's about goal setting, action planning and productivity. In short, it's about getting tasks done. (That's why I like to call it action planning rather than project planning. It implies momentum.)

I've divided the book into four parts to help you stay focused on the process:

- PART 1: Select the best goals.
- PART 2: Choose the right projects.
- PART 3: Create strong action plans.
- PART 4: Get tasks and projects finished.

Throughout this book, you'll be planning your next important projects using the One Action Now system. While we'll focus specifically on the next 12 months, you'll be able to reuse this system for all your projects, tasks, and action planning into the future.

Get into the Groove

If you really want to learn this action planning content, you need to engage your body.

- If you sit and passively read this book, in a month you'll have retained only about 10% of what you read. You will have flushed your time and money down the toilet.

- If you take notes – if you highlight and circle important items on the page – you retain 30 to 40% of what you learned.
- If you physically activate your body, you retain 85 to 90%.

So, don't simply read this material – take notes, discuss it with others, and verbally affirm your intentions. Engage your hands, engage your mind, and engage your vocal cords – these raise your energy level, helping you retain what you learn.

Be a Promise Keeper

Did you know that roughly 33% of all people will break their New Year's resolutions – their New Year's *action plans* – by the end of January?

And 75% will have broken them by the end of March.

It's human nature to make grandiose plans and then, for whatever reason, not be able to implement or stick with those plans.

That's why this book and the One Action Now system is so practical. In Part 1, you'll work on the planning part of your strategy, and then in Part 2 you'll focus on implementation – getting your plan into action.

With a little bit of accountability, you won't become one of those people who break their self-promises in three months. You'll be among the 25% of people who *keep* your promises and *keep* your projects moving forward. That's the whole goal of this book and the One Action Now system.

Your Past and Your Future

Have you ever achieved goals in the past? Of course you have! Take a moment and imagine some of the major and minor goals you've achieved in the past year. You probably completed three or four projects in the past year (maybe more!). You don't need to remember all of them, but remember some of your favorites.

Imagine that all those *past* successes are threaded on a bright white line of light, like a string of beads on a necklace; each *new* success is added to the thread, today and on into the future.

You can know your future by drawing a line through all your key successes of the past. You have completed significant projects before. You can continue to achieve these kinds of successes. Soren Kierkegaard says life can only be *understood* backwards, but it must be *lived* forwards. By examining your past successes, you'll easily determine what works well for you, identify which direction you're headed in, and know that your future projects will also be successful.

If you keep an ongoing I Did It List of accomplishments – big or small, personal or business related – you'll compile a list of fifty or sixty items a year, such as:

- I changed my habit and now keep the sink clean of dishes.
- I took a vacation to Yosemite which I've dreamed about for years.
- I visited my parents more often, enjoying their company and spending relaxing time together.
- I consistently wrote blog posts, a habit I was trying to solidify.
- I designed two new classes that boosted my revenue significantly.
- I researched how to hire a website designer.

Write *everything* down, every accomplishment no matter how large or small. If you're not proud of yourself by the time you're finished writing your I Did It List, I don't know what will make you proud.

By writing this list each year, you've proven a truth: because you've accomplished many goals in the past and you're *destined* to repeat that behavior into your future. The goals you create today are not the stopping point on that big bright white line; they're simply new beads on the thread, now and into your entire future. You've done it before, and you'll do it again.

What have you achieved in the past 12 months? Go ahead, write them down on the I Did It List on the next page.

✗ WORKSHEET

I Did It

In the past year, I accomplished these goals and projects

One Action NOW

Get my free One Action Now Journal with fillable PDF versions
of all the forms in this book.

Visit **www.oneactionnowbook.com/bookresources**

I

GOAL SETTING

1

CAPTURE THOSE COMPELLING GOALS

You have big goals and dreams. You cherish them. You ponder them during the day and hug them close to you at night. But if you keep them all in your head, they hatch like rabbits and spawn even more big ideas and task lists until your head feels full and fuzzy. Let's spend some time uncovering your vital goals and creating a list of what you want from your business (and your life). It's the essential first step in the action planning process.

Don't worry – I'm not asking you to create action plans for all your goals at once. You'll only *start* your goal list now and jot down what you want your life to look like. Take time to contemplate your goals list for several days or even weeks, and add to it a little at a time until it feels complete. At this point, you're simply capturing those goals and putting them in one place.

When I'm setting my goals for the next year, I start by writing them down on a piece of paper. I keep that piece of paper on my desk for four or five days. A new goal will pop into my head when I'm driving the car or sitting in a restaurant. I add it to my list and walk away. It's too soon to judge or analyze the goals on the list and I don't cross anything off the list (yet). I just keep building the list.

This goals list will develop over time. Don't expect that you'll get all your goals on the list in the first ten minutes. Allow the list to percolate through you and ideas will arise. Keep a notebook handy wherever you go!

Goals versus Projects or Tasks

Don't confuse a goal with a project. When you list your goals for the next 12 months, remember that a goal is an *outcome*. It's the result you want.

A project is *how* you'll achieve the goal, a tangible list of tasks in an action plan. Projects are something you *complete;* they have tasks and deadlines.

For instance, say I want to write a book. Writing a book is a project, and I could have many different goals for the book. Perhaps I want to write it to express my creativity, or maybe I'm writing a book to increase my income. In fact, the same book-writing project may accomplish many possible goals at the same time:

- Express my creativity
- Increase my income
- Become known as the expert in a topic

- Enhance my writing skill through practice
- Get my brand out into the world

Just as one project can serve several possible goals, one goal can be achieved by many possible projects. If my goal was to "enhance my writing skill through practice," then all the following projects would serve that goal:

- Write a book
- Write a blog article every week
- Attend a writing class
- Learn a new vocabulary word every day
- Buy and use a thesaurus

See? There are many roads to your goals. The first thing to do is express your goals clearly. Remember, *a goal is an outcome or result you want in your life.* They're very simply stated, like:

- Lose 10 pounds
- Exercise consistently for overall health and fitness
- Increase revenue by 15%
- Double the number of clients we serve
- Get into a serious relationship (or get out of one)
- Take a relaxing vacation in Hawaii
- Have a second child
- Save an extra $5,000 a year towards retirement
- Buy a house

Think *big outcomes.* And ask yourself, "Why do I want this?" and "What's my ultimate goal?"

Write It Down

What are the big goals you want to achieve over the next 12 months? Begin to write those down. Keep it simple. Write a phrase or a sentence that expresses the goal. Base it on the result you want.

If you're not sure what your goals should be, try thinking about all the different categories in your life. Use different Goal Setting Worksheets, one for professional goals and one for personal goals. Professional goals could include career growth or mastering a new skill. Personal goals might include your health, your family and friends, and your personal finances.

Use the Goal Setting Worksheet on the next page and list the goals you'd like to achieve in the next 12 months. Print out this worksheet and leave it on your desk or somewhere handy, so you can add to it any time a new goal comes to mind. (I find that my goals list is ever-expanding. Don't worry too much about it. Just keep writing and we'll worry about prioritizing your goals later.)

WORKSHEET

Goal Setting

My goals and outcomes for the next 12 months

OneActionNowBook.com

First What, Then How

As you're writing your goals, you could be tempted to include the projects that will help you achieve those goals. But don't jump into *how* just yet. Stay focused on capturing your goals and dreams.

It's natural to start brainstorming about *how* to achieve a goal. But it can limit your thinking about your goals list and create blinders that will stop you from seeing the bigger picture.

Let's say my goal is to serve my customer audience as thoroughly as possible. Immediately I start thinking, "I want to have more educational content to share with them." Then I scribble a list of all the ways to create more content.

That's the worst mistake I could make at this point. I either get overwhelmed by the huge task list I've created, or I limit my thinking about the goal itself. Maybe my goal wasn't really to serve my audience as *thoroughly* as possible, but instead was to serve them *more deeply* in a few narrow areas.

Until you comprehend your true goals, creating a task list will send you off in the wrong direction. If you think of a goal and immediately try to figure out how to do it, you could feel overwhelmed and end up crossing that goal off your list prematurely. Worse case, you might not have true clarity about the nature of the goal.

Right now, focus on the *what*. We'll handle the *how* in the How Will You Do It? chapter later in the book.

2

WHAT'S MOST IMPORTANT

How will you choose which goal to work on first? Identifying your values – your criteria for what's important in your life – makes all the difference. First, you'll write a huge list of goals. Then you need some way of judging each goal to decide which ones are the top priority in your business.

The way you make any decision, whether it's about which goals are significant or which computer to buy, is to apply a set of criteria. What are you looking for? What features and benchmarks must be satisfied to make this a good choice? What's valuable to you?

The concept of the What's Most Important Worksheet is simple. In the first column, list all the possible criteria for determining what's important in your business. In the example chart on the next page, I've given you 25 possible benchmarks of what makes a perfect and authentic business. Feel free to add your own; the example criteria are certainly not comprehensive.

In the next three columns, rate these criteria on how important they are.

Then, using the same chart model, you can create criteria for your personal life as well. What makes a perfect and authentic personal life? It can be values like, "I have enough money for retirement savings and giving to my favorite charities" and "I spend time in nature" or "My professional life mirrors my personal values."

Here's an example of a What's Most Important Worksheet for a small business owner.

©2018 Karyn Greenstreet | OneActionNowBook.com

WORKSHEET

What's Most Important

CRITERIA FOR	1 NOT VERY IMPORTANT	2 IMPORTANT	3 HIGHLY IMPORTANT
Work is intellectually and emotionally satisfying		X	
I make more than a livable profit; I make enough for savings, spending, charities, etc.			X
My business mirrors my personal and professional values			X
I help large numbers of people		X	
I help individual people, one at a time	X		
I get my message out			X
I create passive income streams		X	
My business vision inspires me			X

✗ WORKSHEET

What's Most Important

CRITERIA FOR	1 NOT VERY IMPORTANT	2 IMPORTANT	3 HIGHLY IMPORTANT
I expand past my local region, serving people nationally/internationally			X
I have balance between my work life and my personal life		X	
My revenue stream is stable			X
I build a large business with many employees and much revenue		X	
I build a business I can ultimately sell			X
The business culture supports and motivates my employees			X

The concept of the What's Most Important Worksheet is simple. In the first column, list all the possible criteria for determining what's important in your business. Here's a list of 25 possible benchmarks of what makes a perfect and authentic business. Feel free to add your own. What's most important to you?

- I make a livable profit
- I make more than a livable profit; I make enough for savings, spending, gifting, charities, etc.
- My business mirrors my personal and professional values
- I help large numbers of people
- I help individual people, one at a time
- I work with groups of customers
- I get my message out
- I create passive income streams
- I get to use lots of creativity in my work
- I collaborate with people
- I can work alone
- Work is intellectually and emotionally satisfying
- There are a large variety of things to do
- I outsource work I don't want to do, or don't have time/skill to do myself
- I work as many or as few hours as I want
- My business vision inspires me
- Through my work, I feel like I'm living my true calling in life
- I explore and reach my highest potential through the work I do

- I build a large business with many employees and much revenue
- I serve those in my local community
- I expand past my local region, serving people nationally/internationally
- I help people/organizations who will deeply benefit from my products and services
- I have balance between my work life and my personal life
- My work gives me many opportunities to learn new things and explore new ideas
- My revenue stream is stableI call them criteria; you might call them values or benchmarks. It doesn't matter what word you use – it's the way you'll judge what's most important to you.

In the next three columns, rate each criterion:

- **1** is not very important
- **2** is somewhat important
- **3** is highly important

WORKSHEET

What's Most Important

CRITERIA FOR	NOT VERY IMPORTANT 1	IMPORTANT 2	HIGHLY IMPORTANT 3

Identify Your Why

The next thing is to define *why* you want each of these goals. Sometimes we write down goals and we don't really understand the motivation behind them.

- What will this goal do for you, emotionally, physically, mentally, or socially?
- Why do you want this goal?

As an example, Eve, one of my mastermind group members, says she wants to have a more dynamic website for her yoga studio. Why?

Joe says he wants more physical flexibility and strength. Susan wants to have more fun. Tom wants to increase revenue by 50%. Why?

By understanding your motivations, you can choose major goals you will stick with, even if they are long-term goals.

For example, one of my big goals this year is to write two books. If each book is 40,000 words, those are huge goals. It could take me an entire year or more to write and publish two books, including launching a marketing campaign around each one. With a massive long-term goal like that, I might start running out of steam, or hit some potholes in the road to writing and publishing success. Then I might say to myself, "Oh, I have got to give this up! What was I thinking? This is just too hard to do!"

Sometimes you struggle to achieve your goals. Projects can become frustrating or they consume a lot of time. However, if you understand *why* you want to achieve that goal, and if you write it down and put it somewhere so you'll see it every day, you'll keep motivated and stay the course.

This is where being part of a mastermind group with your business peers can be helpful. Other members understand your goals, and why you want them, because they're in the same boat as you are. They're there to encourage you and make sure the tasks you're undertaking are the right tasks at the right time, so you reach your goal. They also help you when you get stuck, because they've been there before, and they have ideas and best practices to shorten the learning curve. Consider tapping into your colleagues as you do this One Action Now process.

Your Goal Isn't Selfish

I want your *why* to be essential and important – *to you.*

Don't think, "Oh, that's selfish," or "The rest of the world won't think that's important, so I should ratchet back what I want out of life."

Be a little self-centered here. It's okay to want to achieve your own goals, and feel you deserve your success. As a human being on the face of this planet, you have a right to have goals and dreams. You're not here to write down your goals and then judge them or belittle your dreams.

Instead, ask yourself honestly: What do I really, truly want?

When Your Why Won't Work

When you write down the *why* for your goal, if you don't feel excited about it, you won't remain motivated. There are only three reasons your *why* isn't electrifying to you:

- **The *why* isn't important enough to you.** You're holding yourself back by choosing easy goals, or your goal is more important to someone else than it is to you.
- **The *why* is so important to you that you're afraid of failing** – so you resist wanting it so much. You dull the energy around it.
- **The *why* is important and you're afraid of succeeding** – and everything that comes with maintaining that level of success.

If you find yourself thinking, "That's not really jazzing me," ask yourself, "What *would* make it exciting enough that I can't wait to get started?"

Sometimes we resist writing down even one goal, much less the *why* for that goal. People have told me, "I'm really afraid of failing, so I don't even want to do this exercise. If I write down this goal and write down the *why*, and then I *don't* achieve it, I'll hate that it didn't happen."

It's a natural response. I have a list of 25 big business goals for the next 12 months. I am afraid that some of them won't happen. I hate not having them happen – I'm one of those people who *loves* to check things off my list. Achieving my goals and keeping my promises to myself are two of my core values.

You must get over that fear of not achieving a goal. Tell yourself, "If I don't want it badly enough, then it definitely won't happen anyway. *I've got nothing to lose by writing it down.*"

Are Your Goals Achievable?

Look at your list of goals. Are these achievable goals? Do these goals seem like something you can accomplish?

If you must learn something new to achieve a goal, can you learn that skill or topic? The answer is probably yes. You have been learning all your life and with the proper teacher, you can learn practically anything.

If the goal means you need to get help, or change a habit, can you do that? Of course you can! It will take willpower and flexibility, but you can do it.

Is this goal reasonable? Have other people been able to accomplish this goal? If other people have already achieved it, there's no reason why you can't achieve it, too. And even if no one else has ever attempted it before, do you feel it's something *you* can do?

Or is the goal so far out there (like living on the moon) that the likelihood of achieving it is low unless you have *amazing* skills and resources? (Unless I've got tons of money and hire a private NASA scientist, it's unlikely that living on the moon is a reasonable goal for me.) Looking at the practicality of the goal is just as important as looking at the possibility of the goal.

You want your goals to be realistic and challenging at the same time.

Challenging but Doable

Here's the test I use to check if my goals are on target: is the goal *both* challenging and doable?

Challenging feels like the hair on the back of my neck stands up a bit at the thought of tackling that goal. *Doable* is that feeling deep in the center of my being that I *know* I can do it.

Being on this edge between challenging and doable is a wonderfully motivating place. If a goal is too challenging, you might believe the goal is impossible, and you will limit yourself through self-defeating behaviors. If a goal is too easy, too doable, you might not put all your skills, talents, and resources into it. Perhaps you'll procrastinate because you think you can get it done quickly, right up against the deadline. Either way, self-talk and self-defeating behaviors rob you of the chance to get what you want out of life.

Use this test on each of your goals and see what results you get. Is your goal challenging *and* doable?

Now, Make Your Goals More Specific

When you're writing down your goals, make them specific and measurable. Don't simply write, "Have more clients." Instead, write, "Acquire 25 new clients in the next 8 months." Be as clear and specific as possible.

How will you be able to judge whether you've accomplished your goal or are close to accomplishing it? If it's too vague, how can you discern whether you've achieved it or not?

Ask yourself:

- How many?
- By when?

As an example, Tom runs a copywriting business and thinks content marketing will help him attract new clients. His states his goal as, "I want to showcase my thought leadership and create video content to grow my business." How much content? Is it three new videos a month or three new ones a week? How many new clients? Two or twenty-two? When is the deadline for achieving this goal? By next month, or by the end of a year?

Psychiatrist Ari Kiev, tells us that having clear goals make problem-solving easier. He says, "Helping people to develop personal goals has been proven to be the most effective way to help people cope with problems." He has observed people who have mastered adversity and summarizes his findings, "From the moment they decided to concentrate all their energy on a specific objective, they began to surmount the most difficult odds." When you're struggling, creating a goal and moving forward helps overcome the difficulties.

SMART Goals

There are five aspects of goal writing that help clarify what you want and how you'll judge whether you've actually achieved that outcome.

As a way of evaluating your goals, I recommend the "S.M.A.R.T Goal" formula:

S = **Specific**

M = **Measurable**

A = **Achievable**

R = **Realistic**

T = **Time-framed**

Specific – You'll accomplish more if you are very specific and clear about your goals, and can communicate them to your team. Answer the questions: Who, What, Where, How, and Why? Write your goals so that others can easily understand them.

Measurable – You can't track the progress of your goals unless you include quantifiable numbers or milestones. How will you measure your progress and your ultimate success with this goal?

Achievable – Set goals that are reasonable and doable. You can self-sabotage your success by setting goals that you can't reach with the time, skills, or resources available to you. We'll talk more about managing project resources later in the book.

Realistic – Are you both willing and able to work towards this goal? Do you believe you can reach this goal? You must know, deep in your heart, that this is possible.

Time-framed – Set a deadline for the completion of your goals and for all smaller milestones along the way.

To illustrate, let's talk about Eve who runs a yoga studio. Her current location doesn't fulfill her needs. It's small and crowded. There are few windows and it feels dark inside. She can only run one class at a time and there isn't enough parking. If she wants to grow her business, she needs a larger space to rent. One of her goals is to have a new, dynamic yoga studio location that will appeal to more people. I asked Eve:

- Who are you trying to attract?
- What does "dynamic" mean to you? How will you know when your yoga studio is dynamic?
- How many people are you trying to attract?
- How many classes do you want to run simultaneously?
- When do you want to have the new yoga studio up and running?
- What's the general area where the yoga studio will be located?
- Do you need more than one location?

If Eve is specific about her goals, it will be easy for her to identify when she has reached them. Eve's updated goals look like this:

By December, I have opened my new yoga studio in the downtown area, with a nearby free parking lot. The studio has two classrooms, plus an entry area, public bathrooms, and private offices, all brightly lit and painted warm, energizing colors. Each day we run nine different classes: three during the morning hours, two in the afternoon, and four in the evenings. We double our client base, attracting more professionals who want to attend classes in the evening. Clients and staff alike report feeling empowered and embraced by our positive, healthy studio culture.

Where SMART Goals Fail

There are times when SMART goals will cause bottlenecks and barriers. Here are common problems with SMART goals so you don't get trapped:

- **Your vision or your project (or business) is too new.** When you're at the very beginnings of a new venture, you don't know what you don't know. It's too soon to set specific goals and deadlines because you haven't thought it through completely. Perhaps you don't know which resources will be needed and when they'll be available. More research is needed before you can set SMART goals.

- **You focus exclusively on the short-term goal, and lose sight of the long-term vision.** For example, you want to increase your revenue, so you create a new six-week marketing campaign project with specific targets for reach and revenue from that campaign. That makes sense, right? But if you focus all your energy and resources on that one six-week campaign goal, you're missing the bigger picture. What's next after the six-week campaign? What are other ways to increase revenue in the long-term?

- **Some things you simply can't control.** No matter how well you plan, you can never plan for the unexpected. And you can never control what other people will do, even if they have a contract. Despite this, I encourage you to persevere! Without a plan, you're doomed to struggle or fail. SMART goals might take a pounding when the unforeseen occurs, but you'll be skilled enough to rework your SMART goals in the face of change.

- **Missing a deadline can put you off the project entirely.** No one likes to miss a deadline or a milestone, but sometimes it happens when your project plan meets reality. It's disheartening when dates whoosh by or your to-do list gathers dust. Will you abandon your project at the first setback?

- **It's all an educated guess.** You can't always pinpoint which deadlines are appropriate or which goals are possible. When planning, you'll do the absolute best at estimating your SMART goals, but other projects and priorities may get in the way. Making wise decisions every day plays a huge role. When you're clear on the outcomes you want and why you want them, you can look at the SMART goals for all your active projects and decide which are the most important to work on today.

Goal Setting Worksheet Revisited

Now that you appreciate that *why* is just as important as *what*, revisit your goals list and add the motivation and the specifics. Fill out the Ultimate Goals Worksheet and answer these questions:

- Why is this goal *crucial*?
- Why do you want to achieve this goal *now* rather than sometime in the future?
- Which goals will be in alignment with your values? From

the What's Most Important Worksheet, add your
motivators to your goals list.

- What is the specific goal, the desired result, and the
  deadline?

One Action NOW

WORKSHEET

Your Ultimate Goals

My goals and outcomes for the next 12 months

GOAL SPECIFICS AND DEADLINES	WHY THIS GOAL IS IMPORTANT

✂ WORKSHEET

Your Ultimate Goals

My goals and outcomes for the next 12 months

GOAL SPECIFICS AND DEADLINES	WHY THIS GOAL IS IMPORTANT
Increase revenue by 50% by Dec 31	This allows me to hire more staff, which leverages my time, making the business more scalable.
Showcase my thought leadership	This puts me out in front of my target audience on a regular basis and attracts new prospects.
Two hundred new students by December 31	This increase revenue and provides introductory students who will become advanced students
An overall marketing system in place that's repeatable	This allows us not to struggle and re-create every launch campaign from scratch.
Provide incredible value to my students	This creates satisfied customers (fans!) who purchase more from us and tell others about us.

One Action Now Checklist

Before moving on to the Priorities chapter, have you:

- Completed the What's Most Important Worksheet?
- Completed the Ultimate Goals Worksheet, including using SMART goals features like deadlines and specifics?

3

PRIORITIES: WHICH GOAL FIRST?

Let's figure out which of your goals are crucial to creating the business you want. Make sure you've completed the What's Most Important Worksheet so you have criteria you'll use to judge each goal.

Next, we'll circle back to the goals list and ask, "Which of these goals will best help me create a perfect professional or personal life?"

I use this phrase very deliberately – the *perfect* life.

Why shouldn't you have a perfect business or a perfect personal life? Don't settle for a life you don't want or a business that isn't a clear reflection of your dreams.

It's fine if you don't like the word *perfect*. It's a tough word and can bring up resistance, fear, and cynicism. You're welcome to use the word *authentic,* which means, "I'm honoring myself, and this is what represents a true personal and professional life for me."

Will you achieve this mythical perfection? You're much more likely to have exactly what you want if you write it down and/or tell other people about it. If you don't invest time to figure out what a perfect life looks like for you, you will stumble in the dark and achieve only half of it.

When Eve was working on her yoga studio expansion, she was nervous about setting big goals and designing a perfect life. Her life was far from perfect. Juggling a business and a family made her feel scattered. Money was always an issue. And choosing to expand the studio meant she had to give up other goals that were important. When she paused to consider what a perfect life looked like, she divided it into several categories: her perfect business day, her perfect family situation, and her perfect financial life. When she set the criteria in each of these areas and decided what was optimal, she could choose goals which flowed in that direction.

If there are people integral to your goals (perhaps people who define and share your goals with you), include them in this exercise. They, too, will have input on what a perfect business partnership or family relationship looks like. Now is the time to hash out any differences in goals or values, before you make critical commitments to undertake a vital project. If there's disagreement on the goals, you may find they argue about which projects to work on or openly sabotage the project work itself.

Let's go back to your goals using your criteria. Which goals will help you to create a perfect life and which goals won't?

Sometimes you can't be sure. You must take an educated guess about your most important goals, and ask: which ones feel the strongest to you? Which ones will get you the results you want?

But What About All My Other Goals??

In my One Action Now class, participants struggle to narrow down their goals to only the crucial ones. How can a few be "crucial" when *all* of them feel so important, so necessary?

I'm not asking you to ditch all your other goals. Instead, I'm asking you to focus on the ones that matter most today, and use those goals as you learn the One Action Now system. Then you can go back to other goals and put them through the system, too.

How you make that decision – and all the other decisions you need to make in your business – depends on the criteria you select. More importantly, decision-making depends on what's going on inside your head and heart.

How to Avoid Making Dumb Decisions

Decisions and business go together; you can't escape it. Every day your business demands you to make decisions. Sometimes you have all your facts in front of you and you make a wise decision that skyrockets your business upward. But are all your decisions wise ones?

A bias is a disposition (mostly unconscious) to make decisions based on illogical grounds. Everybody has biases, which are based in previous experiences, beliefs, cultural norms, and personal values. They tint your thinking and, therefore, the decisions you make. Once you recognize your own biases you can work to overcome them and choose the best goals for you and your business.

When choosing your most important goals and the projects to reach those goals, here's some brain science to make you smart about where decision-making fails.

Framing Bias: Are you framing the goal as "How do I avoid loss?" or do you say, "How do I gain more?" It's two sides of the same coin that can lead to vastly different options and decisions.

You are influenced by the way a situation, problem, or goal is described– so you make decisions based on that definition. Instead, ask:

- Is this the best way to frame the question?
- Is this really the foundational goal?
- How is this problem or decision connected to other things?

Hindsight Bias: Your past doesn't always equal your future. However, when you've had an unfavorable outcome in the past, you tend to avoid similar situations where you might repeat that failure. You're concerned that you didn't learn from your bad experience, so you avoid any whiff of the same circumstances because you're fearful you won't know how to make it work this time.

The opposite is also true: it's believing that recent success and good fortune will continue into the future. Remember, at the very start of the Great Depression, people invested more than they could afford to lose because of their belief that stock market prices, having risen in the past, would always continue to go up. They borrowed money to invest in the stock market. When the stock market crashed, they had huge debts and no way to pay.

Part of this hindsight bias stems from paying too much attention to highly dramatic events from the past, either big wins or big losses. Your brain keeps track of any event that's associated with an extremely positive or negative emotion. These can skew your decision-making by giving them more weight than is appropriate. Putting these high-emotion events in context stops you from distorting your memories.

Intuition Bias: There's nothing wrong with trusting your gut. After all, where do you think intuitive decisions come from? They come from your past experiences, beliefs, knowledge base, and worldview.

But as we've seen with other biases, your past experiences don't always give you a full picture of what to expect in the future, and unexamined beliefs, cultural norms, and your own emotional needs can cause you to create goals that *feel* solid but actually are not.

Emotions must play a part in any decision-making. We often set goals because we want to feel a certain way (either wanting the specific outcome, or the emotional fulfillment about having *finally* decided on a goal instead of sitting on the fence about your goals). But don't let emotional needs make you assume your intuition is strong. Be self-aware enough to look at all aspects of the goals you select instead of going with your gut alone.

Weighted Criteria Bias: You pay more attention to one or two decision-making criteria, giving them higher weight than they should have. Imagine you are making decisions on buying a house. One criterion would be price. Other criteria would be location, number of bedrooms, layout of the house, nearby shopping, etc. What if you gave more weight to the number of bedrooms (because your growing family was experiencing great pain from lack of space and privacy), and that led you to purchasing a house for more than you could afford? This is why identifying your values and decision-making criteria is crucial to selecting sound goals and creating intelligent action plans.

Overconfidence / Over-optimism Bias: You are overconfident when you believe your own knowledge, decision-making skills, capacity, and/or capability are bigger than they actually are. Then you carry unnecessary risks and set stretch goals that are beyond what's possible. I'm a huge fan of stretch goals, if they are prudent.

Sometimes you overestimate your ability to manage any bad outcome of a poor decision. You think, "If it doesn't work out, I can figure out a way to solve it." Or it can take the form of overestimating your ability to predict future events accurately.

If you're a naturally confident and positive person, this bias will require you to step outside yourself and ask, "Is what I believe about myself and my abilities actually true?"

Prudence Bias: Like overconfidence, prudence is an extreme belief. It's the tendency to be overcautious.

If each piece of your goal or project has a little wiggle room in it, "just to be on the safe side," you compound the cautiousness of your facts and estimates, and make inferior decisions. While it's good to create a worse-case scenario so that you can manage all possible outcomes, weighing your decision towards being overly cautious can remove options.

Anchoring Bias: When you generalize first impressions, you can attach to them as "the starting point" without analyzing whether the first pieces of information are accurate or are an appropriate starting point in your deliberations.

For instance, what if your vendor told you that, "All of these machines start at $400,000." You will then believe $400,000 is a normal (anchor) price for every machine you look at, even if the truth is that they regularly sell for $350,000.

When choosing your most crucial goals, don't gravitate towards the first ones you've written on your worksheet. Writing each possible goal or project on an index card, and shuffling them, might help you to avoid anchoring bias.

Selective Perception Bias: We've all done it: seeing what you *want* to see and failing to see other options. It's called tunnel vision, or looking at information with blinders on, and it affects what you're willing to pay attention to.

You'll see this happen in certain industries or certain peer groups: there are expectations about how things "should" work, and those limitations cause you to stay focused in that narrow band and not look outside it for the bigger picture or better options. When you hear, "We've always set our goals this way," it's time to step outside the selective perception and find new ways of looking at both the goal and the possible ways to achieve it.

Confirmation Bias: In this bias, you've already reached a conclusion and then you try to find the facts to justify it. Have you ever known someone who tries to make the facts fit into their conclusion? A person buys a sweater that is highly over-priced, and then justifies their purchase by saying, "It was the last one! And I'll wear it all the time. And when will I ever get back to that shop again?" That's confirmation bias.

Normally you get facts and information first, *then* you make your decision. Confirmation bias is the other way around: You see what you want to see, and you justify your decisions with a narrow set of facts, ignoring all other facts.

Imagine you're ready to make a big decision to pull the plug on a major project. If you call up a colleague who had made a similar decision, the conversation will be biased towards making the decision to cancel the project. The opposite is true: if you speak with someone who decided to *not* stop their project, the conversation could be biased to encouraging you to not stop your project, too.

Having your own peer advisory board or mastermind group made up of people who are unrelated to your decision (and not emotionally invested in it) can help you get many points of view. Ask them to play devil's advocate and look at all sides of the goals you're setting.

Pick Your Crucial Goals

Now is the time to make a commitment: choose one goal you'll work on throughout the rest of the One Action Now system. Next, select supplementary goals that you'll achieve as a natural outcome of working on your One Crucial Goal.

One Action NOW

✖ WORKSHEET

One Crucial Goal

I WILL WORK ON THIS ONE CRUCIAL GOAL

BY WORKING ON MY ONE CRUCIAL GOAL, I WILL ALSO ACHIEVE THESE GOALS

One Action **NOW**

✖ **WORKSHEET**

One Crucial Goal

I WILL WORK ON THIS ONE CRUCIAL GOAL	BY WORKING ON MY ONE CRUCIAL GOAL, I WILL ALSO ACHIEVE THESE GOALS
Showcase my thought leadership	By choosing to showcase my thought leadership, I'm expanding my reach, getting known, and driving traffic to my website. It gives me the basis to talk about my classes, and to introduce my copywriting system in a unique and valuable way. These free videos are the on-ramp to all my marketing, so the more traffic they drive, the more revenue I'll bring in. In short, this one goal will greatly assist nearly all my other goals.

II

PROJECT PLANNING

4

CREATING YOUR PROJECT
WISH LIST

I get it – you're creative and you have a million exciting projects you want to work on. Now that you've narrowed down your goals list, I bet you're already thinking of projects.

So, let's work on your Project Wish List. This is a list of all the ideas and projects you'd like to start over the next 12 months.

Don't worry right now about tying these projects to any specific goals; just create a list of projects you've been wanting to pursue. (You know, the ones that are sitting on your shoulder, whispering in your ear!) You'll select the most worthwhile projects later in the One Action Now system.

Write down *everything* you dream about accomplishing, every project you've been pondering. Maybe you won't ultimately choose to do each project on your Project Wish List, but the point is to get it out of your head and on to paper. That's why I call it a *wish list* instead of a *to-do list*: it's a place to store all your project ideas, everything you can dream of doing.

Here are some ground rules:

- **Don't worry if the list isn't complete.** Allow time for your thoughts to percolate and new project ideas to arise, and write them on your Project Wish List over the next week. If your team is involved with project selection, do this exercise with them, creating a team Project Wish List.

- **Don't judge your list.** Write your project ideas without judging the merits of an individual project or how long it will take. Maybe you won't get every project completed in the next 12 months – some might need more than a year. And don't cross items off list because you don't think they're possible.

- **Don't worry about *how* you'll do each of these projects.** You limit your Project Wish List by jumping immediately to the *how*. For now, write out the wish list of *all* your projects and ideas.

- **Be as creative as you can.** What are all the projects, no matter how crazy or impossible, you could do that would help you to reach your goals? This is a great question to brainstorm with your team, colleagues, or mastermind group, because they can add other inventive, inspired ideas that you hadn't contemplated.

Use the Project Wish List Worksheet on the following page to start capturing your ideas.

One
Action
NOW

WORKSHEET
Project Wish List

✕ WORKSHEET

Project Wish List

To reach my One Crucial Goal,
I could do any of these projects:

Create a 52-week free video
tutorial series

Write a book

Create a class on advanced
copywriting

Speak at conferences

Create an online self-study
program

Teach at a local University

Conduct live webinars

Show before and after examples
on Facebook and LinkedIn

Write and offer a free ebook

Be a guest on an influencer's
blog or podcast

One Action Now Checklist

Before moving to the next phase of the One Action Now system, have you:

- Written a Goals list, being as specific as possible?
- Determined your *why* for each goal?
- Selected criteria for a perfect business and what's most important to you?
- Chosen One Crucial Goal you'll work with for the remainder of this book?
- Created a Project Wish List of all the projects which could help you achieve your One Crucial Goal?

Do not go forward until you have these items completed! Trust me, if you don't compete these now, you'll make inaccurate decisions later which will cost you time and money.

In the next part of the One Action Now system, you'll start connecting the dots between your Project Wish List and your One Crucial Goal, and prioritizing both so you can select the projects to work on.

5

NARROW YOUR FOCUS

Let's narrow down your Project Wish List and pick one project to start planning in detail. If you're like me, you have 20 or 30 projects on your wish list! I'm asking you to focus on *just one project* while we walk through the One Action Now project planning process.

Of course, you'll be able to use this process repeatedly with each of your projects. In fact, this week a student emailed me and said she was still using the planning worksheets from One Action Now – four years after she had attended my class. To learn and master the system, select a project to use while reading this book. Later you can apply it to all your projects and goals.

The One Action Now system – along with creating a mind map, which I'll address later – is how I *always* do my action planning. When you have too many ideas circling around in your head, you tend to feel overwhelmed and you can't identify which to tackle first. When you get those ideas out of your head and onto paper, clarity suddenly emerges. Write down one idea and your mind automatically thinks of other connected ideas. Having a central location to store your thoughts helps you to see the big picture as well as all the details and how ideas or tasks are related. (Keep these worksheets on your desktop or wherever you can access them quickly, because you'll return to them and add ideas as time goes by.)

Tackling Multiple Projects is Killing You

I'm just like you – I have a million ideas and I want to do them *all* right away!

I learned an important and enlightening lesson last year that I'd like to share with you: by focusing all my attention, energy, time, and resources on One Vital Project, I increased my income – and more importantly, I was happier and more relaxed.

I was shocked! Even though experts had been telling me for years to focus solely on one project, I didn't want to give up my freedom and creativity. I liked having multiple projects to work on. It made me feel vibrant and alive.

But it also made me feel unproductive, cranky, overwhelmed, and a nervous wreck. And guilty, because I was having a hard time completing just one of those projects to my satisfaction.

Imagine you are driving down a busy highway at rush hour. Now imagine that there are three other people in the car with you, all trying to have a conversation with you simultaneously. Now your cell phone rings. In between all this talking, ideas pop into your

head so you pull out your mobile device to type in some
text notes.

Crazy, right? You'll have a car accident any minute now.

Yet that's exactly what you're doing to your business when you try
to focus on multiple projects or multiple goals simultaneously.

Multitasking Myth

In the 1740s, Lord Chesterfield said, "There is time enough for
everything in the course of the day, if you do but one thing at once
– but there is not time enough in the year if you will do two things
at a time."

They knew about multitasking back in the 1740s!

Performing more than one task at once doesn't get more done, and
it doesn't make you more efficient. Recent studies by several
research teams prove this point.

According to researchers at the University of Michigan, when you
toggle between multiple tasks, you are using what's known as the
"executive control" process. This mental CEO chooses priorities
and allocates thinking/creativity resources. The more you switch
between tasks, the longer it takes to re-focus attention and
resources. (In fact, we're never really doing two tasks at once.
We're switching repeatedly *between* those two tasks, so the proper
term should be "multiswitching," not multitasking.)

David E. Meyer, a cognitive scientist at the University of
Michigan said in a recent New York Times article, "Multitasking
is going to slow you down, increasing the chances of mistakes."

When it comes to your business, mistakes will cost you. Can you afford to lose time or money?

On a practical level, working on multiple projects simultaneously made me feel scattered and out-of-control. It diffused my intellectual and creative abilities. When I slowed down and focused on one major project for two full months, four amazing things happened:

- I felt more in control.
- I was much more relaxed.
- My confidence soared.
- I was able to get the project completed *a full four weeks ahead of schedule.*

It was as if I had been released from a multitasking prison of my own making. Talk about freedom!

Consider the effect your own multitasking is having on your project success. Is it time to change your habits?

Tying Your Goals to Your Projects

Go back to your Goal Setting and Crucial Goals Worksheets. Out of all the goals you have, which ones are the most important?

Now look at your Project Wish List. Are there one or two vital wish list projects that will help you to achieve those goals?

As an example, say that a pivotal goal is to drive traffic to your website. There may be five or six different projects that could help achieve that goal, but only one that achieves it *best* or with the *quickest results*.

Start connecting the dots, looking at each wish list project and connecting it to the goal(s) it will help to achieve. Some projects may help you achieve two or three goals at the same time, which is amazing. There's efficiency in working on one project which achieves multiple, simultaneous goals.

Remember Tom, the copywriter? Here's an example of how Tom compared his goals to his projects:

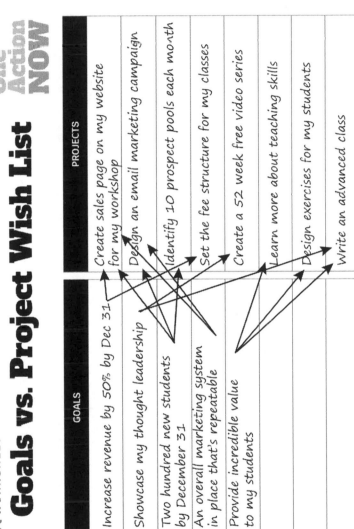

Goals vs. Project Wish List

One Action NOW

GOALS

Increase revenue by 50% by Dec 31

Showcase my thought leadership

Two hundred new students by December 31

An overall marketing system in place that's repeatable

Provide incredible value to my students

PROJECTS

Create sales page on my website for my workshop

Design an email marketing campaign

Identify 10 prospect pools each month

Set the fee structure for my classes

Create a 52 week free video series

Learn more about teaching skills

Design exercises for my students

Write an advanced class

©2018 Karyn Greenstreet ‖ **OneActionNowBook.com**

Goals to Projects List Worksheet

Go ahead and tie your goals to your projects. Some connections will be obvious. However, some might take a bit of re-thinking: are you limiting your connections because you only perceive your projects from one point of view? (This might be a good time to brainstorm this with your team or a colleague for some outside critique.)

WORKSHEET

Goals vs. Project Wish List

One Action NOW

GOALS							

PROJECTS							

Narrow It Down to One Vital Project

Once you've completed the Goals versus Projects exercise, begin selecting your best project – your One Vital Project – to work on next. Ask yourself:

- Which project will most likely produce the outcomes from my goals?
- Which project will strategically lead me and my business in the direction I want?
- Which project am I ready to tackle now?
- Which project inspires me?
- Which project scares me?

Choose One, Master It, Move On

Selecting One Vital Project has the biggest impact on the success of your business.

If it scares you to limit yourself to one project, ask yourself why. Are you giving up something important by narrowing your selection? Are two of your values competing with each other?

Tom had two projects that seemed crucial to him: designing a sales page on his website to market his classes, and implementing a market research project to discover what his students wanted to learn. Each project would take him over eight weeks to complete, and sixteen weeks seemed like too much time slipping away. Even though each project would have a positive impact on his goal, he had competing values: he enjoyed (and was good at) writing sales copy for his website, yet the market research work gave him confidence about his class offerings.

I reminded him that he didn't have to focus one project for four months and bypass the second project. Instead, he could focus on the first project for a month, and see what results he got. This serial approach to projects allowed him to test the waters, tweak along the way, and still leave room for additional projects once he finished the first one. By focusing on the market research project exclusively, he completed it two weeks early, and could begin the website update with a clearer vision of his customers' needs.

You can tackle multiple projects in one year, but be smart about it. First, choose one project. Finish it. Then move on to the next.

Emotions of Your Choices

Face it, some projects are exciting and some projects are drudgery. If you try to decide on your One Vital Project solely through the lens of your intellect, you miss valuable emotional insight that may impact the success of your project later.

Let me share an example from my own business. I had a big goal I was working on: Write a book to promote my business and establish myself as an expert. I had three projects to choose from (let's call them Project A, Project B, and Project C) – any of which could further my progress towards my goal.

But when I talked about Project C, there was no energy in my voice – and my mastermind group told me so! Out of the three projects, Project C was the *absolute best one* to move towards my goal fastest. However, I had done that kind of project so many times in the past, and it wasn't interesting or fun anymore. I could do that kind of a project with my hands tied behind my back; it wasn't challenging for me.

My mastermind group know that one of my values is to have challenging, interesting work. Pamela said to me, "Instead of deleting Project C from your list, *why don't you find a way to make Project C more challenging and exciting?*"

This caused an entire mind shift for me. It had never occurred to me that I could frame the project in any way I wanted *beyond what I would normally do*, so that it could both serve my goals and my values simultaneously. My limiting beliefs about the way the project "should" be done stopped me from choosing it, even though that type of project had been successful in the past for me. A little creativity can transform a project and fulfill your values and needs on many levels.

Look at your project selection through the emotional impact lens, and ask yourself these four questions:

1. **Which of these projects energizes you?** Which project really excites you? You'll keep motivated and finish the project if the project itself is interesting and challenging. Tom was most excited about writing the sales page for his website.

2. **Which projects *need* to get done?** Some projects aren't exciting, but they're important to complete. Be willing to work on projects that aren't very exciting, but are very, very practical and will yield massive results. Strategically, Tom needed to identify what his customers

wanted before he wrote his sales page. It wasn't exciting work, but it needed to get done.

3. **Which projects will help you achieve your most important goals?** You'll be frustrated working on a project that doesn't move you towards your goal. Even if that project is vastly successful, if it doesn't give you the *outcome* you desire, you'll wonder why you spent time, money and other resources on it.

4. **When reviewing an individual project, where in your body do you feel it?** Is it tickling your intellect or touching your heart?

Not every project is a passion project; some projects simply need to get done. But if you could have both – excitement and practicality – why not go for it?

I had to readjust my thinking of what Project C entailed. I was faced with the dilemma of choosing Project C, because intellectually, financially, strategically it was the best choice. But as I had envisioned it, it was boring and rote. So I went ahead and *multiplied* the project – made it bigger, more challenging, and more exciting. I designed the project so it would ask me to reach deep inside to pull out strengths. For me, expanding the project to allow me to learn and use new skills (one of my core values), and to work with a larger, worldwide audience (another core value), made the newly redesigned Project C the perfect project to work on. As a side note, I've been working on Project C – taking The Success Alliance to new heights – for three years now and am still invigorated by it every morning!

For Tom, the choice was clear: strategically he had to do the market research first. It was the gateway to building his business and serving his customers. Conducting market research tasks wasn't appealing, but the outcomes sure were. When he reframed the market research project based on the deep information he'd receive, it became more palatable.

Look at each project on your Project Wish List. If you're not enthusiastic about some of them, but they're an excellent project that's sure to achieve your goals, ask yourself:

- How can I redefine or redesign this project?
- How do I expand it or reshape so it becomes a project I'm excited about?

Go Ahead, Choose Your One Vital Project

For the sake of learning the rest of the One Action Now system, choose one project you're willing to commit to. You will certainly tackle more than one project over the next year, but for now, select just one. Afterwards, you can apply what you've learned to all your projects via the One Action Now system.

What is one project you truly would like to get done in the next 12 months? If you could get only One Vital Project done – one that excites you and you've been itching to work on – what would it be?

I will focus on this One Vital Project:

_____

_____

III

ACTION PLANNING

6

HOW WILL YOU DO IT?

W e've looked at what you want to accomplish, and the reasons why these goals and projects are strategic for your business. You've chosen one project to dive into. It's time to start creating your project *action plan*: a list of the tasks necessary to complete your chosen project, along with task deadlines, and resources needed for project.

Having a task list is essential. Each task represents a step towards completing your project. Writing down these tasks is the first phase of designing your full action plan.

Tom needed a way of tracking the topics that were interesting to his students. So, he created a project to produce a series of short, educational videos about copywriting to attract new clients and students. I asked him, "Is this free content you want to create? Or, do you want to also create paid video workshops as well?"

When he said "Both," I reminded him that he was talking about *two separate projects*. I asked him to focus on one project, and he chose creating free videos, which would allow him to do market research and build his reputation as a copywriting authority at the same time.

Next, we began to brainstorm his tasks, or *how* he would create these videos. He realized he had to choose a topic, research what he wanted to say, write a script, record the video, edit the video, upload it to his website, and then announce the free video to the world.

When he listed these tasks in a logical order, he saw that there was a well-defined, linear path of tasks to complete his project. There was clearly a first step, second step, and so on.

Not every project has a linear path. Say that I want to write all my blog posts for a year, in advance. I've decided to sit down for two solid weeks – eighty hours – and write all my blog post for the entire year. I'm not required to write any specific blog post first. I can write on any topic I want, in any order I want. The rule is that I get them all written in the two-week window I've allotted for the project.

For your One Vital Project, what are all the tasks you need to complete to finish that project? Record your tasks on the Task List Worksheet. Don't worry about organizing them for now, just write down your ideas.

One Action NOW

✕ WORKSHEET

Task List

Create Sub-projects

When you are listing tasks, you might notice that some tasks can be grouped together under one heading. I call this a sub-project, or a milestone. It's helpful for you to see your project laid out in an outline form, especially if you're a visual person.

Tom's project, including his three sub-projects, might look like this:

Video Project
1. Pre-Work
    a. Choose five topics
    b. Write a script
2. Recording & Editing
    a. Set up the video and lighting
    b. Record the videos
    c. Edit the videos
    d. Upload them to the website
3. Marketing
    a. Write an email announcing the free videos
    b. Send the email to his mailing list
    c. Write a blog post about his free video
    d. Add the blog post to his live blog and share it on social media

I encourage you to write your task outline on a word processor or note-taking software so you can easily insert or delete tasks, and reorganize tasks under different sub-projects as necessary.

Selecting Your Action Planning Tools

Whichever tool you choose to map out your action plan is fine – there's only one rule: *Will you use that tool daily?*

If it's hard to update, or not easy to access, you won't use it. Make sure you choose a tool that works for you and get in the habit of updating it consistently for everything you need to capture. For instance, I keep my action plan on a clip board next to my phone. That way, I know exactly where it is and I can refer to it often.

Below are some action planning tools which help you stay organized.

Tool: Mind Mapping

Mind mapping is a visual planning tool rather than a linear planning tool (like the list on the previous page). The idea is simple: start with a piece of art paper or flip chart paper, or use a whiteboard. Whichever you choose, you want a big, blank, clean surface.

In the center of the page or board, write down and circle your project. From the central project title, draw lines for each task you must do. Add tasks to the mind map wherever they seem to fit best. This gives you a visual representation of your project – then you can create a linear task list from the mind map.

Here's an example of Tom's project in a mind map format. In this first draft, he simply added the tasks as he thought of them; later he can re-arrange them into sub-projects or the order in which he'll complete each task.

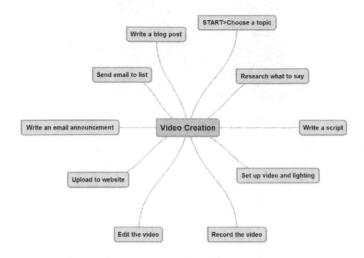

Mind mapping is a powerful, flexible tool when you need to get it out of your brain first, then figure out the details later. Afterwards, you can organize your map, deciding which tasks come first, or how long each task will take.

I like to use an art pad – about 12″ x 18″ or larger – because I can carry it around with me and add to my mind map whenever something comes up. When I'm working with my team, we use a whiteboard so we can all make notations and see the big picture together. (Have you heard of dry erase paper rolls? These are self-adhesive rolls of dry erase film which you can attach to any wall – instant white board! We use the Prefer Green brand.)

Mind Mapping Resources

If you're techie-minded, there are mind mapping software packages that allow you to create a mind map. Using software, you can easily create and update your mind map as you work on your projects.

On YouTube, you'll find simple video tutorials on how to create a mind map. Look for the tutorials from Tony Buzan, who pioneered the mind mapping technique. It's helpful to watch as a mind map is being created, and you'll immediately comprehend the techniques when you watch someone else do it.

Go to the One Action Now Resources website to get free access to the mind mapping software list and the links to recommended mind mapping tutorials:

www.oneactionnowbook.com/bookresources

Mind Mapping Sub-Projects

As you mind map your project, you may discover that your giant project can be divided into small sub-projects, which makes task planning easier.

Here's an example of what Tom's project would look like if he were to divide his task into sub-projects visually:

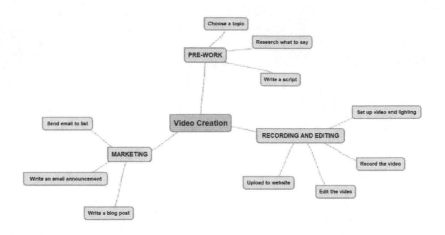

Tool: Gantt Project

Another project-planning tool I use is called Gantt Project (it's free). Gantt Project allows you to take a basic task outline, like the one Tom created, and expand it by adding start dates and how long each task will take. You can actually *see* on a chart when each task starts and ends. You can see if you've got too many tasks going on at one time (like the three tasks on the far right all occur on the final day).

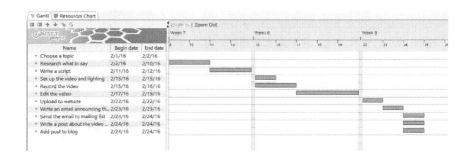

I don't enjoy juggling multiple task lists or bits of paper with "to do" items scribbled on them. By using software like Gantt Project, you can create an overarching action plan for your project with all the necessary tasks and timing. The chart quickly tells you if you're overloading yourself and your team.

If you've assigned too many tasks to a particular day or week, change the start date of some tasks and move them to the following week. This flexibility and practicality will make action planning easier.

Tool: Monthly Task Calendar

If you prefer, you can add all your tasks on a blank calendar with the same effect. It might look something like this:

You can either use a calendar in your computer (like in Microsoft Outlook), or buy a month-at-a-glance calendar at the local bookstore or office supply store. Hint: If you use a paper calendar, I recommend you get one with a matte finish to the paper, so you can use a pencil and erase when necessary. If you get a calendar with a glossy finish, it's hard to write on it in pencil. Trust me, a pencil is your best friend when it comes to action planning. It reminds you that nothing is permanent while you're in the planning process.

Juggling Multiple Projects

As you begin mapping out your first project, you might get excited and want to map out *all* your projects. That's great! I love your enthusiasm. And I encourage you to use these tools to put all your projects in one place so you can grasp the overarching puzzle of managing your time and resources among projects.

Some people like to focus on one project at a time. Others enjoy having multiple projects in the works simultaneously. I've already discussed the reality of trying to tackle too many projects at once – the more projects you work on concurrently, the longer each project takes (unless you're outsourcing the entire project to someone else).

But there are times when you will be working on two or more projects at the same time. For each project, complete an individual Task List Worksheet. If you want to see all your projects and tasks in a central location, consider building a Gantt project or a monthly calendar with all projects on it. You could color-code the tasks for each project to see both the big picture and each individual project on the same page. As the business owner, you need these types of dashboards to grasp what's going on in your business.

If you're working on multiple projects at the same time, you'll probably outsource the work to other people (either delegating tasks to someone on your team or hiring consultants). By using Gantt Project, you can create a resource chart, identifying which person is responsible for each task. It makes your supervision of the project easier.

If Gantt Project is too techie or cumbersome for you, consider a simplified version. Grab a piece of blank art paper or flip chart paper. Lay out each project in a its own box, with the tasks to complete *that week* under each project heading, like this:

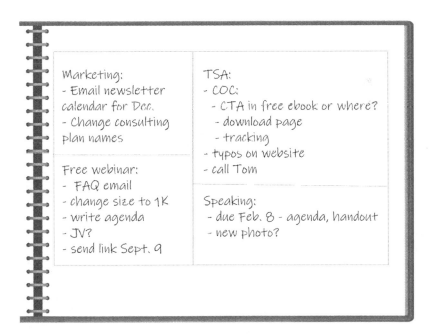

That way, it's all on one sheet of paper, and you can update it weekly. Again, write in pencil or use a word processor to create this chart. When a task is done, you can erase it from the page. That gives you space to write in the next task to be completed.

In this way, you won't get so focused on one project that you forget about the others, and you can see at a glance the interplay of tasks.

One Action Now Checklist

Before moving on to the What's Most Important chapter, have you:

- Completed your Task List Worksheet?
- Used one of the tools (lists, mind mapping, Gantt charts, task calendars), to write down all the tasks associated with your project?
- Organized your tasks into logical groupings or sub-projects?

7

TOOLS, KNOWLEDGE AND RESOURCES

W hen Tom was talking through his video project tasks, he reminded himself, "Oh, I need to get a new microphone." As he brainstormed his Task List, additional resource needs surfaced.

What tools, knowledge, and resources (TK&R) do you need to get your tasks done? Do you own them and have them at your fingertips, or do you have to acquire them?

Tools

Tools are physical products and systems that help you complete a task. In Tom's case, his tools are his camera, his teleprompter, and his video editing software. He realized he needed to get two more important tools: a new microphone and a green screen.

Knowledge

Knowledge (and skill) is the ability to get a task done. Sometimes you have that knowledge already. Other times, you need to learn (or master) something before you can attempt a task. If you don't have the time or inclination to learn that piece of knowledge, then you need to outsource that task to someone else.

Tom had done some video production in the past. One of his tasks is to create a graphic for the first screen of his video, which has the name of the video and his website URL on it. Tom doesn't know how to create graphics like this, and he doesn't want to learn. So, he'll contact a graphic artist to get this graphic designed, then he'll add it when he's editing the final video.

Resources

Resources are what you need *in addition to* knowledge, skills, and tools. For instance, Tom needs to buy a microphone but he doesn't know which one to buy. However, he has a colleague that he can contact to ask for suggestions on the best microphone. The microphone is of course a tool, but the colleague is a resource.

Resources also include time and money. How much time will this project utilize, and where will you find that time on your calendar? And if you need to purchase something, how much money will it cost and how long will you have to wait for it to be delivered?

Don't forget your team. Whether you have employees or you outsource tasks, these people are an incredible resource that leverages your ability to complete projects and reach goals. Do you have a team in place? If not, how will you acquire this valuable resource (and where will the money come from to pay them)?

Why Worry About TK&R Now?

At this point in the planning, you might be itching to jump in and start getting things done.

That can be a terrible mistake!

Imagine you write your script and set up your video camera, only to discover you forgot to get a microphone. Now you get sidetracked by researching which is the best microphone, and then you have to purchase it. That means driving to the store or waiting for a delivery. Acting too soon slows you down.

In advance, think of the exact order the tasks need to be completed. List the TK&R needed to accomplish each task. When it's time to start the work, you can focus without distractions or disruptions. *Advanced planning speeds your progress tremendously and makes completing your tasks more efficient.* It's about doing the right thing at the right time, knowing all the steps in advance.

The TK&R Homework

On the following worksheet, list all the tools, knowledge, and resources you'll need for your project. Go slowly, reviewing each task individually, so you don't miss any important resources the task will require.

This is the place where you write, "I need to brainstorm with someone about this task," or "I need to join a class to learn more," or "I need to hire a consultant to get this task done."

Include things like:

- What to research
- What to learn
- What to outsource/delegate
- What to buy
- What money you need
- Where will you get the money from
- Which tools you need
- Which systems or processes to put in place
- Where to add the tasks to your calendar (or your team's calendar)

Create a high-level outline of these on the Tools, Knowledge and Resources Worksheet – a reminder system for you of what you need in place before you can complete a task.

WORKSHEET

Tools, Knowledge & Resources

One Action NOW

TASK	TOOLS, KNOWLEDGE OR RESOURCE NEEDED

✕ WORKSHEET
Tools, Knowledge & Resources

One Action NOW

TASK	TOOLS, KNOWLEDGE OR RESOURCE NEEDED
Outline what I'm going to say in each video.	Look in online notebooks and hard drive for saved notes around each topic.
Make notes in the scripts where images are inserted in the video.	Do we have these images already, or do we need to make them?
Discuss lighting needs, which microphone to use.	I know we need a new microphone. Do we have everything else we need for filming?

8

TIME AND MONEY: YOU CAN'T ESCAPE THEM

N ow is the time to start taking action. But before you jump in, add each task on your calendar or Gantt chart, and take an educated guess about how long each task will take to complete.

Why? Because time is a resource, and you want to use it wisely. Calculating task duration allows you to determine if you're making appropriate progress, and identify when the project will be completed.

Certain times of the day may be more productive for you than others. For example, I'm really bright in the morning for creative tasks. I can write a 3,000- word chapter for my book in a few hours in the morning – and it would take me *twice that time* to write it in the afternoon.

My intellectual stamina seems to drop after 3:00 p.m., so I don't put arduous tasks in my calendar from 3:00 to 5:00. Instead, I use that time for simple, relatively mindless tasks.

When is your best time for getting things done each day? You understand your own mind, body, and the way you work best.

Another calendar consideration is this: when is the best time of year to work on a massive project? For many business owners, things slow down during the summer months or in November/December, so that's a good time to work on a big or complex project. Note that I said *work* on a giant project – you should have done the planning *before* the slow times of the year, so you can jump into action immediately when you have the time. Many businesses do their annual planning in December so they can jump in on January 2.

It's not always possible to schedule big projects for slow times of the year, but if it's an option for you, consider it. Are there typical times in your business or industry when things are busy and when they're slow?

Big Blocks of Time

If carving out a few hours here and a few hours there doesn't work for you for whatever reason – your calendar doesn't function that way or your business doesn't run that way – consider taking a huge block of time *away from work* (like a whole week!) and getting your entire project done in one big chunk.

When writing books and preparing new classes, I find that taking an entire week or ten days away from the office allows me to complete the project all at once. I simply don't schedule client calls, teach any classes, or run any mastermind groups for that entire week. No team meetings, no phone calls, and emails only twice a day.

If I'm willing to concentrate all my energy on that single project in one big block of time, instead of it taking three or four months I can complete it in just one week. There's something special about all that focused time and, frankly, it's a joy to focus on one project for an entire week. For instance, I'm editing this book during the week of Memorial Day in the USA. It's a slow week anyway, so I put aside all other projects and work to focus on getting this book finished.

If you are looking to get an important project done, and you can carve out that large chunk of time away from your daily work, that's great. You must set some ground rules, though. How often will you return phone calls and emails? Will your team be allowed to interrupt you, and if yes, when can they do it?

For me, the first time I did this, it was a huge ah-ha moment. Where had this been all my life? Once I discovered this secret, I've been using it consistently for several years. One time we rented an offsite meeting room for a few days so that we could complete our annual strategic plan. We schedule three-day retreat weekends with my mastermind group so that everyone can work on the big picture of their business away from the everyday distractions.

I was recently talking to an literary agent about a new book, and he asked, "How long will it take you to write your book?" I said, "Four weeks." He said, "What? Are you kidding me?" I said, "Four weeks, every day, 40 hours a week. 160 hours of solid writing. I write a thousand words an hour, 90 hours for the first draft and 70 hours for editing the second draft."

He was skeptical. "Wow. Can you really do that?"

I said, "Yes, *because I have to.* I don't have time to write a 200-page book using only one hour a day. That would take me two years — and it's simply not worth it if it takes that long to get a book out. If I can give the project my full attention for 160 hours, solid time back-to-back, I'll do it."

If you can work in big chunks of time, and that appeals to you, it's a sound way to budget your time.

I discuss more about time management and mindset in Part 4 of this book.

Pick Three Tasks

A colleague shared a great tip a few years ago: instead of writing a huge to-do list every day (and never completing all the tasks), she selects just three tasks a day to focus on.

I've been using this technique now for several years, and I'm happy to report it is a winner! Each day, I choose three tasks to complete. If I finish them, I can always do a fourth task.

For some reason, having only three tasks a day feels infinitely more empowering. I'm able to do them easily, without feeling stressed or overwhelmed. Now I'm moving forward in my business at a faster pace.

Try it and see if it works for you, too.

Budgeting Your Money

It helps to plan your money requirements when working on your action plans. Say that Tom's new microphone costs $200, and the graphic design work costs $600. Maybe he needs to attend a class on video editing to sharpen his skills (and make him more efficient at video editing, which is a worthwhile investment). How much would that class cost?

Your project financial needs will vary – some projects cost a little bit of money, and others require a hefty investment of cash. You need to add the money element to your list of the resources for your project. You certainly don't want to run out of money mid-project because you didn't budget for it, right?

Here are some possible expenses:

- Outsourcing tasks or hiring a consultant
- Buying a book or taking a class
- Buying equipment or software
- Taking time away from paying work

We often forget about the *opportunity cost* – the income you could lose while your time is being spent elsewhere. If you need to reduce the time you spend with clients, or reduce the amount of marketing you do so the money can be invested in your new project, what revenue loss might be incurred?

WORKSHEET

Project Cost

What are the specific financial costs associated with my project?

One
Action
NOW

✕ WORKSHEET

Project Cost

What are the specific financial costs associated with my project?

Carole, Lee and Kathy already on payroll.

Kathy working on multiple projects, so might have to pay her some overtime for a month or two ($1,000 – $1,500).

Need to purchase microphone (under $200).

Might need to upgrade video hosting plan to the next higher level to hold all these videos. (Increase of $50/month ongoing.)

Depending on whether we host the Learning Management System (LMS) ourselves or rent space on a public platform, there will be an additional cost plus we need to hire someone who knows how to set up and manage an LMS. Total estimated first year cost: $8,000.

(Add a task: determine which LMS we're going to use and the cost. Add a task: find an expert who sets up and maintains LMS systems.)

Double-check Your Work

Review your Task List Worksheet and your Tools, Knowledge and Resources Worksheet. Are they complete? Are you ready to start moving forward and designing your full action plan?

For some people, working on these worksheets depresses them. They say, "Oh, where am I supposed to find the time? Where will I get the money?"

The intention of these worksheets is not to dampen your spirit or cause you to feel overwhelmed – it's to be realistic about what's necessary for completing this project.

When you've completed these worksheets, you've honestly thought about what this project will require. You will recognize if it's worth doing and what kind of commitment you'll need to make to complete it.

One Action Now Checklist

Before moving on to the 90-Day Action Plan chapter, have you completed:

- Task List Worksheet (or however you've captured all your tasks)?
- The Tools, Knowledge and Resources Worksheet?
- Project Cost Worksheet?

9

YOUR 90-DAY ACTION PLAN

Once you've amassed your task list, you may discover that your project could take many months to complete. Some projects take longer than others, and you need to remain flexible in your action planning for the year. As you know, the unexpected always turns up, and delays can shoot holes in the best plans. To manage this, a three-month planning horizon is the perfect chunk of time for action planning purposes. It's long enough to get even the most complicated task finished, and short enough that you can envision the horizon as it comes up to meet you.

Once you write your Task List for a project, look at which tasks you can truly accomplish in the next three months. Which projects do you expect to work on, and which tasks (and projects) will you complete in ninety days?

Pick one project and at least three tasks you'll get done in the next three months. Then, go back to your Tools, Knowledge and Resources Worksheet, and determine which of those items you need to have in place so you can complete the 90-day tasks.

You might find, as an example, that you have a large learning curve in front of you, and you must master that topic before you can seriously work on your project. Say you want to enroll in an online class on that topic, but that class will take an entire month to complete. If you need to devote a month to taking the class, don't add too many tasks to that same month. Be honest about what you can accomplish and how long tasks will take.

Consider Your Personal Plans, Too

While we're talking about mapping out your next ninety days, don't forget other commitments. If you have a vacation planned, or need to spend time with your family, make sure you've accounted for that time on your calendar.

You might say to yourself, "I can get this done by the end of December!"

Then, you begin to realize there are personal plans to consider as well: "Oh, yeah, my family is coming here for Thanksgiving weekend, and then I have to travel to my in-law's house during Christmas week. Then, New Year's week we're going skiing." In other words, there are three weeks you're *not* going to work on your project during a six-week period.

Capturing Your Tasks in Detail

We're about to go on a wild ride!

By now, you've begun to realize that you can't do a million tasks at once. It's up to you to choose the most important tasks and get into action.

Look at your Task List. It may seem daunting to complete all the tasks. Here's a hint that will reduce your anxiety: *break down tasks into singular actions you can take.* I use the term "action" here because it has power. A "task" feels bland and perhaps a little threatening. But an action feels empowering. An action says: *do it!*

What is *one important, tactical action* you'll commit to completing, and when will you do it?

Using the One Action Worksheet, add that one action into the slot of the specific week you'll accomplish it. If an action needs more than one week, write it into as many weeks as is appropriate.

If you find that an action is spanning too many weeks on your action plan, it may be that this isn't simply one task: it can be broken down into multiple, smaller actions. Look at each task and ask: Can I break this task into simpler, doable actions?

For instance, Tom's task is to "Edit my video." He thinks it will take two weeks to complete. This one task can be broken down into smaller component actions, each one taking just a few minutes or a few hours:

1. Export the video from the camcorder into the computer.

2. Import the video into the video editing software.

3. Watch the entire video and identify cuts that need to be made.

4. Edit the video and cut where necessary.

5. Create transitions where the cuts have been made so that it's easier for the viewer to watch the video.

6. Add the title graphic to the front of the video.

7. Render the video to create a final output version.

If Tom divides his bigger task into its smaller component actions, he can add each of these seven mini-actions onto his calendar. Now he's scheduled time to get each one completed.

Go ahead and add your actions to the One Action Worksheet. Consider each task carefully and make sure you believe you can get it done in one week. If the task seems too big, divide into smaller actions.

Are you sure you can succeed at that task in the assigned timeframe? If your answer is a weak, "Yeah, I *guess* I can get it done," that's a signal that you're not sure. When you are *certain*, you'll invest much more energy and more of your potential into a task because you believe it's possible to complete it successfully. Not simply to complete the action – but to get it done in the time you think it will take.

If you're not sure you can get a task or action done in a week, try this trick: double the time you think it will take. If you think it needs three hours, write *six hours* on the One Action Worksheet.

It doesn't hurt to overcompensate when estimating how long a task

will take. If you get done early – that's great! But remember
Murphy's Law – an old adage that says what *can* go wrong, *will* go
wrong. If for some reason the task work is not flowing naturally, or
if there are errors or problems, you've built into your plan some
Murphy's Law time – time for things to not go well. I'm not trying
to be pessimistic here, just realistic.

How Long Does a Task Take?

Unless you've done similar tasks before, you often must make an
educated guess about how long it takes to complete a task.

Chunking a task down into mini-actions significantly helps with
estimating task duration. If you estimate a task will consume 20
hours, it's probably more than one action. Constantly ask yourself,
"Can I divide this up into smaller actions?"

For example, say that I have a task to write a chapter for my book. I
estimate it will take me two hours. But wait a minute – that's two
hours to do the actual writing, but there's more to the task than
writing the final copy. I must pick a topic and outline what I want
to say. There might be a little research I have to do before I can
begin writing – and then I have to write it. And I need time to put
it aside and let it cool off, come back the next day, and edit it. All of
these are mini-actions under what appeared to be a simple task,
"Write a book chapter." Turns out this task has five actions and
demands closer to five hours of work, not two hours.

If you're having a hard time figuring out how much time an action
will take, tease it apart to identify every single step within that

task. If you've never done this action before, do some research online or ask a colleague to help you estimate the timing.

Remember: Challenging but Doable

Earlier in the book, I talked about the idea of a task being "challenging but doable." Find the balance between a task that's challenging (it requires a bit of work to get it done) and a task that's doable (you are confident, deep inside, that you can accomplish it).

Here's why: If it's too challenging, you might sabotage yourself. If it's too doable – if it's too easy – you might sabotage yourself as well.

If it's too easy, you can mess up your action plan and calendar by assuming you can get something done in 15 minutes when it really takes two hours. (Remember the Overconfidence Bias from earlier in the book?) Conversely, you can sabotage yourself by thinking, if something is too hard, perhaps you shouldn't bother starting it at all.

For each task (or smaller action), week by week, ask yourself, "Does this feel challenging? Does it raise the hair on the back of my neck?" It's great if it does!

Then ask yourself, "Do I feel it's doable? Have other people done it? Do I know other people who have done it? Can I get help, support, and guidance on how to do this? Or, can I figure it out myself? Do I really, truly feel it in my gut that I can do this? It stretches me, but I can actually complete this action?"

If you can answer yes to those these questions – whether an task is challenging and whether the task is doable – you have created a perfect task for yourself because it excites you and you will be continually motivated to move forward. It won't be too easy, and you won't underestimate how much time or effort is required. That's the perfect balance you want to achieve when you're creating your action plan.

Business owners don't always work alone on projects, and your team might not agree on your assumptions. You might consider a task challenging but doable, and your team doesn't feel the same way. You must consider their skill set and their mindset, plus their time constraints, and ask clarifying questions to uncover what might be causing the resistance. If the entire team isn't onboard with this action planning work, it will come back to bite you later.

One
Action
NOW

WORKSHEET
90-Day Action Plan

WEEK 1 TASKS	WEEK 2 TASKS	WEEK 3 TASKS

©2018 Karyn Greenstreet   OneActionNowBook.com

✂ WORKSHEET

90-Day Action Plan

WEEK 1 TASKS	WEEK 2 TASKS	WEEK 3 TASKS
Choose a topic for the next 5 videos.	Convert the outlines to scripts.	Carole to set up the lighting and microphone, and test both.
Outline what I'm going to say in each video.	Make notes in the scripts where images are inserted in the video.	Carole to set up the teleprompter and test.
	Review the script with Carole. Discuss lighting needs, which microphone to use, post-production needs.	Shoot the first video and review together as a benchmark for all the others.
		Carole and Lee review first video.

✄ WORKSHEET
90-Day Action Plan

WEEK 4 TASKS	WEEK 5 TASKS	WEEK 6 TASKS
Shoot the other four videos. Give them to Lee for editing.	As Lee gives us each video after it's edited, Carole and I can review the final output. Once approved, Carole can upload the final version. Start to map out a marketing campaign, with each technique and timeframe. Pick a launch date.	Write the introductory blog post. Write the email campaign. Give email copy to Kathy to put into the campaign funnel system. Choose which segment of our mailing list to send the campaign.

Feeling the Resistance Yet?

If doing this detailed level of planning makes you want to jump off a cliff, I understand.

Do you remember how awkward it was to learn to drive a car? All those steps and controls and pedals to push! It's the same with learning action planning. Soon you'll master this skill and it will become second nature. You're learning a new way of thinking, and training your brain to work more efficiently. You're teaching your brain to complete your planning *before* you get into the action. Like every important skill you've had to master in the past, it can seem awkward at first.

You're training your mind to divide big projects into smaller, doable actions. You're learning to assign actions to a specific block of time. You're teaching your mind to consider what's truly possible to accomplish. If you find this is stretching you beyond what you are comfortable with, understand that the resistance you're feeling is because you're asking your brain to think differently. Remember the amygdala? It's feeling stressed, and it shows up as resistance.

It's time to have a little talk with your brain: "Listen, we'll work on this together. I'll support you in every way I can, and you're a smart brain – you can figure this out. I understand it feels uncomfortable and different in the beginning, but it will get easier over time, I promise." You might feel silly talking to your brain, but try it just once, and feel your whole body relax.

There are two wonderful videos about resistance by Barbara Sher.
Consider watching them if you are resisting doing your action
planning, or even choosing a project to work on. Check out the
One Action Now Resources website for these videos:

www.oneactionnowbook.com/bookresources

IV

TIME MANAGEMENT AND MINDSET

10

GET INTO ACTION: WHAT'S STOPPING YOU?

Y ou've journeyed with me through all the steps needed to set up a One Action Now plan. But this effort can be squandered if you aren't vigilant in defending yourself against those big time-wasting tides of modern life and the unexpected forces that disrupt your day.

When Eve was visiting possible locations for her new yoga studio space, her office manager called her cell phone: the wind had blown the tiles off the roof of their existing studio and rain was pouring in. Eve quickly called her real estate agent and cancelled the walk-throughs, and hurried back to the studio. There she found everyone, staff and patrons alike, mopping up the floor and hurriedly emptying buckets. It took three frustration-filled weeks to reschedule the walk-throughs of the new studio space. Some crisis or critical task always took precedence. Her best laid plans had gone far astray.

Sound familiar?

In the remaining portion of the book, I suggest strategies to protect and defend your One Action Now plan against these harmful currents. Unforeseen circumstances derail us. People want your attention and you can't focus on your important projects and goals. All too often, you procrastinate or choose actions that won't lead you towards success.

11

THE GRIM REALITY OF ACTION PLANNING

I do big-picture thinking and major project planning for my business once a year, often in the summertime or in December. I review those plans monthly and ask:

- Have I changed what I want from my business (or personal life) which would rearrange my goals?
- Are the projects still in the right priority order?
- Have new priorities or projects arisen?

I revisit and revise the action plans often: they're *living documents* because my business is a living business that breathes and morphs as situations arise and goals shift.

Think of your project planning process, and your action plan document, as a *living document*. It's intended to change and evolve as you work with it; it breathes. Businesses by their natural are every-changing, and sometimes priorities get re-arranged. There's nothing inherently wrong with saying, "I plan to work on this particular project in June," and when June rolls around, you realize your priorities have shifted.

The project which you scheduled for next month might take a backseat to something more important or urgent. Be aware of *why* you're changing your plans. If you are actively making a wise decision about moving a project start date because priorities have changed, that's okay. If you're constantly procrastinating and putting projects off because you feel like they're too huge, or they're too much of a challenge, or you don't know where to start, it's time to re-evaluate your mindset.

The Myth of Available Time

The feeling of being overwhelmed is rampant. I see it everywhere: my business colleagues and clients complain of it, and I see it among my family and friends as well.

The myth they keep repeating to themselves is, "You can always get more money but you can't get more time."

The truth is, you *can* get more time. You limit yourself when you say there's only one way to manage your time. Time management is about checking those tasks off your action plan *in whatever creative way you can*. You can do it yourself, you can automate it, or you can delegate a task to someone else.

Sometimes the way to manage time is to manage which tasks get on your action plan in the first place. Ask yourself, "Why is *this task* on my list in the first place? Why am I the one assigned to this task?" If the answer isn't sound, you can delegate the tasks to others, or (gasp!) delete it entirely. You have complete control: you can add tasks to your action plan, and you can modify your action plan to fit your strategic goals.

Time management isn't only about scheduling tasks into your calendar; it's about big picture strategic thinking around your entire personal and professional life. Without identifying your goals and values, your vision of how to invest your time is confused and contradictory. If you don't have clarity about *why* you're doing tasks in the first place, you can't identify what to work on, what to delegate, and what to throw away.

12

OVERCOMING PROCRASTINATION

(DON'T SKIP THIS CHAPTER)

We can't talk about productivity without talking about procrastination and why you don't get things done – even when you have a well-defined action plan for your project.

Why do you put off tasks? Even when you schedule them in your calendar, even when you know that tasks to do and why you're doing them, something stops you from moving forward.

There are many reasons, and here's a list of what my clients have told me about their own procrastination:

- "Sometimes I know I procrastinated on things that I didn't like doing or I felt like they were going to be a big deal to do. I often find that once I get into them, they're *not* as big as I feared. So, I try to remember that as a way to not procrastinate. I tend to build things up in my mind and the effort to get started feels much bigger than it actually is."

- "I just think some tasks are boring."
- "I enjoy the energy of having something to do. I feel disappointed when I get a task done because now I don't know what to do with my time. It's kind of having this thing egging me on. It fabricates a false kind of energy, having a big to-do list."
- "I get really excited about having an action plan, and the number of tasks expands. Then, it gets overwhelming. That excitement from having a manageable task list just gets blown out when there are 55 tasks on that list."
- "I think it comes down to passion. I can get up first thing in the morning to go catch an airplane and go on vacation, or get up early in the morning to go skiing or fun stuff like that – stuff I can get excited about. If there's no passion there, I can't get fired up about it. Until I find something within those tasks that brings passion to the task, then it's just going to be a tedious thing that needs to get accomplished. I have to recognize why I'm doing something and I have to want to get to that goal."
- "A fear of success, fear of failure, fear of ridicule, fear of being overwhelmed."
- "I like the adrenaline rush I get when I'm up against a deadline."
- "There are other things I'd rather do."
- "What if I fail?"

You look at tasks and attach some negative possible outcomes to them, whether that's realistic or not. Sometimes the fear is well-founded. Let's face it, it *is* possible that your project might fail. It *is* possible that you might stumble during your work on a task.

Be truthful with yourself. "I'm not motivated" or "I'm afraid" is *not* an excuse to avoid working on an important task. You can spend a lot of time in analyzing your motivations – or you can deal with the reality of having to get the task done if you want the project to succeed. Only you can determine whether a thought is limiting you or whether it's a truly important strategic factor when planning your project work.

Remember the Amygdala?

In the first chapter, I told you about your amygdala, that part of your brain that wants to keep you safe. If you frighten it or stress it, it sends signals to your body that encourage survival – which frankly means avoiding doing anything you find difficult or challenging.

How do you step around the amygdala? How do you *not* wake it up? Design tasks that are tiny and non-threatening. Choose tasks that keep the sleeping giant asleep.

When you're looking at your task list, you might see something like, "Create a video," and immediately you think the project looks too daunting, with too many tasks involved. You might even worry that you'll fail.

The minute you hear this type of self-talk, pause and consider: What's *one tiny step, one single action you can do now,* that will start you on your way to creating your videos?

Perhaps the tiny step is to go to the store and purchase a microphone. Another tiny step is to grab a piece of paper and start jotting down video topic ideas. These are miniscule tasks. These are non-threatening. These won't wake up your amygdala. After you complete that small task, find another small task. Eventually, you get the entire project done using these little steps.

When you break down your projects into tiny, doable tasks that feel like they're possible to accomplish, your amygdala does not get triggered, and your flight or fight response does not go haywire. You get to use all your creativity and all of your logical mind without that resistance to getting things done.

When you find you're resisting a task, it's probably because you're thinking too big. What's the next tiny, tiny step you can take? What's the *one action* you can do *now*?

Simple.

Keep peeling away the onion of tasks until you get down to a miniature action that's doable, that feels safe. There will be some tasks that are outside your comfort zone, but when you look at a project and you take *one action now*, these actions build up over time, and you get your project done.

Let me give you another example. Imagine that your project is writing a book. If you've written a book before, your amygdala says, "Oh, that's okay. We've done this before – it didn't kill us. It's safe. Let's go!"

But if you've *never* written a book before, or you remember writing a book and it was a huge, stressful project, then the prospect of writing a book can trigger your amygdala.

Instead of saying your task is to "write a book," think: *just one action now*. What's one step you can do, right now, that will move you forward? If you set a timer for 30 minutes to begin outlining your book chapters, those 30 minutes feel non-threatening and completely doable.

Linking emotional rewards to a task trains your brain to relax about that type of task. After you've completed an action, remind yourself how much you enjoyed working on that task. (Okay, maybe you didn't *enjoy* doing it – but I bet you enjoyed checking that task off your list, right?) Pause for a moment and revel in the pleasure you feel. Doing so trains your amygdala that these types of tasks produce gratifying feelings. The opposite is also true: when you stress out about doing a task, you train your brain that this task is something to avoid in the future.

Through self-talk and being conscious of your choices, you lay down a neural pathway that teaches your amygdala that this kind of a task is safe. It's enjoyable, it's doable, and it's worth accomplishing. Spending time to train your amygdala pays off big time!

No One Wants to Change the Diapers

Some tasks are inherently boring or onerous, even if the overarching goal is desirable.

Everybody wants a healthy baby, but nobody wants to change a diaper. (Or in my house, everyone wants a healthy cat, but no one wants to change the kitty litter.)

Until you make the connection between the task and the thing you are passionate about, the tasks aren't interesting or challenging – just trivial, dirty, and time-consuming.

When you associate a negative feeling with a task, you naturally resist doing the task again. Worse, you slant your speech about this task towards the negative, so your team picks up the cadence of, "This task is horrible. Let's all avoid it." When someone is asked to do it, they feel they're being punished.

Whether you're talking to yourself or your team, how you frame the task sets the tone. Next time you must change the diaper, you'll coo, "Oh, we want a healthy baby and changing the diaper is an amazing way of keeping Junior healthy!"

Addicted to Research

Joe from one of my mastermind groups recently posed a question: Why did he spend all his time conducting research and never actually *doing* the thing he was researching?

He loved looking up information, finding resources, interviewing people, and gathering facts. But taking these facts and *applying* them to his business – that always got put on the back burner.

It's called *analysis paralysis*. Here's how this thinking shows up: "If I could just gather this information, if I could just find that fact, if I could make this checklist a bit longer…" (You get the drift.) As a small business consultant, I see my clients get caught in this trap all the time, constantly adding new research tasks but never getting into action.

The cause is simple: It's easier for many people to conduct

research than to do the action work, because *gathering research is often a successful task (happy amygdala!)*, while acting on the research is fraught with the possibility of failure, stress, or pressure. You stay in research mode because it's safe and you get lots of positive feelings from uncovering the information you need.

Don't get me wrong, research is vital. I've seen many businesses fail because they haven't done the marketing research necessary to determine what customers want. Business owners don't thoroughly research which vendor to choose, and have to back-track and hire a new one when the first one doesn't work out. But if you spend all your time doing research, and never offering your new product or hiring a key vendor, you'll never achieve your goals.

How do you know when to stop researching? The key, as always, is balance. When you find yourself doing more and more research, you can bet you're procrastinating on the getting-things-done side. You have two choices:

1. Try to figure out *why* you're not taking action, or
2. Just do the work.

Either choice is valid, but guess what? Choice #1 is still research.

Shiny Object Syndrome

There's a growing trend: people are getting distracted by too many ideas or the latest fad, going off in a million directions, and never completing anything. This lack of focus is costing you and your team hundreds of hours a year in lost productivity, lost hours, and lost dollars.

It even has a name: SOS - Shiny Object Syndrome. It's not quite ADHD. It manifests as that new idea which captures your imagination and attention, and you get distracted from the bigger picture. You wander off on tangents instead of remaining focused on the task at hand.

You think of a new idea, you hear of a great new gadget or marketing technique, and *zoom*, you're off on a tangent! There's great energy and excitement in *starting* something new. It feels positive and uplifting. Why do something boring or stressful when you can feel the happiness of new beginnings?

When this happens, everything gets started but *nothing* gets finished. Countless hours and dollars are wasted in pursuit of the new, shiny object without any thought as to whether this new item, technique, service, or product is necessary for you and your business goals.

It's Not Just You

Lest you think that it's only business owners who suffer from SOS, you'll be surprised to find it's rampant in many situations:

- Software and tech companies are notorious for following every cool new fad that comes along, without thinking strategically about whether it's a good fit for their business model. Google Glass might make a comeback, but I'm not betting on it. And I did own a Microsoft Zune...I think it's in a box in my attic.

- Thanks to SOS, TV producers create new shows, then dump them too soon. Sometimes TV shows take a few seasons to find its audience. (I really liked Arrested Development, but wasn't aware it existed until Season Two.) With companies like Netflix, Hulu, and Amazon creating original programming, we'll see SOS show up more often. If a show isn't a hit in Season One, they'll replace it.

- Corporations follows every leadership development fad from new books or leading gurus, only to drop it when the next cool fad arrives. Once popular Management By Objectives (MBO) and Total Quality Management (TQM) have been replaced with or morphed into newer, fresher ideas.

- A homeowner redecorates a single room at a time, but changes styles so frequently, there's no harmony to the entire house. One room is Colonial, the next is Victorian. And the bathroom is Mid-Century.

Tips for Choosing a Focus

Yes, it's hard *not* to get excited about every new idea that lands on your desk. Some of them are very, very cool. But you must stop and ask yourself:

- Is this idea right for my business goals?
- Do my customers want this product or service, and are they willing to pay for it?

- Do I have the time, resources, energy, and money to invest into this project to make it successful?
- Do I have too many open projects that I need to complete *before* I begin something new?
- Do I have the *ability* to finish this new project, implement it, and maintain it?
- What needs to drop off my radar for me to start something new?

There's nothing wrong with loving innovation and reinvention. Just make sure you don't lose focus of what's most important for you, your business, and your customers.

The Pain of Not Doing the Task

People who are successful in their life look at the task that's in front of them and readily acknowledge the potential consequences of *not* doing that task. They're aware of their inner voice that says, "I don't really feel like doing this task right now. I think I'll have a piece of chocolate cake instead because that feels better."

Want to get past the immediate gratification excuse and get moving on your project?

When you *imagine* and *feel* the consequences of not working on a task, you can't rationalize putting it off. You realize that if you don't change the kitty litter, your vet bill will be massive. Fluffy will develop urinary tract infections. You'll take repeated trips to the veterinarian with a howling cat in the car, and you'll have the struggle of sticking pills down a cat's throat for 10 days. Even if you don't *want to* change the kitty litter, you'll go ahead and do it anyway, because having a sick cat and a giant vet bill would be much worse.

If you get the task done, imagine all the good things that will happen as a result! If you find yourself avoiding a task, ask yourself, "What are the *positive* consequences if I complete this neglected task?" Picture an energized Fluffy chasing after a bit of string and jumping wildly in the air to catch it. Imagine Fluffy cuddled up next to you as you read a book, purring contentedly. Clean the kitty litter, and you can be living in this bubble of happiness with Fluffy!

Envision the consequences of your choice far out into the future, as far as you can conceive. Visualize what life will be like if you do the task – and if you don't do the task. This will quickly change your mind.

Write Them Down and Talk About Them

Dominican University of California conducted a study to determine how much people actually get done towards their goals. The researchers asked two questions:

1. Do you write down your goals?
2. Do you tell other people about your goals?

The results were conclusive:

People who *did* write down their goals did better. The study showed that 61% of the people who wrote down their goals accomplished them.

Here's the real eye-opener: People who *both* wrote down their goals and shared them with others were the real winners. An amazing 76% of these people accomplished their goals. What does that tell you?

Write down your goals, your projects, and your tasks. Then share them with someone, especially someone who is willing to hold you accountable for completing them. Whether it's a family member, colleague, coach, or mastermind group, find someone who wants you to succeed and is willing to listen to you as you share your goals. You'll see more clearly through the eyes of another. Outsiders can hold a mirror up and reflect your planning and your mindset.

13

THE EASIEST WAY TO CONTROL YOUR TIME

You've mastered the self-talk and mindset work in the previous chapter. It's all about keeping your focus and committing to your goals. Here are tips to kick into *super-*productivity mode.

Make Productivity Planning a Habit

I strongly encourage you to have a set day and time each week when you plan your projects and tasks for the week ahead. It keeps you concentrated on the goal if you carve out scheduled time to choose priority tasks and get them on your calendar.

Each Monday morning, I design an overarching task list for the week. I look at my calendar to see when I can schedule a task into a specific time slot – essentially an appointment with myself. I review and adjust as necessary. Imagine how energized you'll feel when you start each day with clarity and focus.

Don't overburden yourself by assuming you can do more than what's possible. Typically, three tasks a day is doable. It's more satisfying to schedule and complete three tasks than to schedule five tasks and only complete three of them. If you have more time, you can get an extra task done. And if you don't have extra time, you haven't destroyed your promise to yourself.

When you're adding the tasks on your calendar and weighing what's right for the upcoming week, ask yourself:

- Which goals are these projects related to? What's the big picture? Remember, in Priorities Chapter I encouraged you to select your crucial goals. Now is the time to stay in your lane and keep your eyes focused forward. All tasks should revolve around a crucial goal unless a true emergency arises.
- What projects are these tasks related to? While I'm a big fan of focusing all your attention on One Project, sometimes you'll be working on several projects simultaneously. For instance, your goal might be to hire a new marketing specialist. One project is to find and recruit that person. Another affiliated project is to create a training and onboarding plan for any new employees you hire. Have a clear association of which tasks are for which projects, especially when you're working on parallel projects.
- Why am I working on *this* task? It's easy to get confused and jump into any work that surfaces on your desk. Take

a moment to prioritize your tasks, which ensures you're
chipping away at the most important tasks first. If you
find yourself drawn to doing a task that's not a priority,
it's time to query your amygdala: are you doing this task
because it's easy, it gives instant gratification, and/or it
allows you to avoid a more difficult task that's tickling
your fight or flight response?

By having a set time each week when you work with your task
plan for the week, and habitually asking about priorities, you
exponentially increase your productivity and motivation.

Create a Project Calendar

Getting your projects and tasks into your calendar as real
appointments will change your life. Block out time on your
calendar for your project work and vow to keep that
"appointment" with yourself. And *do* call it an appointment –
you'll take it more seriously and give the work the status it needs.
You wouldn't miss an appointment with your doctor or
accountant, so why miss an appointment with yourself?

Here's a great way to work with a project calendar:

1. Use a month-at-a-glance calendar for the entire year. I
   encourage you to write in pencil. Trust me, you'll be
   making edits to this calendar until you're satisfied with
   the results, so erasers become your best friend!
2. Cross off all the holiday weeks and vacation weeks – weeks

you know you won't be working, or weeks your customers will be distracted by their own vacations, industry conferences, etc. (If you don't know the habits of your customers, now is the time to do some market research.)

3. Cross off the days and times you can't do project work because of other commitments. For instance, if you always have team meetings on Tuesday mornings, cross those time slots off your calendar.

4. Mark your project deadlines on your calendar, including interim milestone deadlines. Indicate when you want to complete your project. Remember Eve who sought to move to a bigger location? She wanted to have a Grand Opening for her redesigned yoga studio on September 15, so she marked that on her calendar. That way, she could work backwards from that date for her task planning.

5. Pencil in the tasks on your calendar in the appropriate order. If you plan to send an email to your customers referencing a specific website page, you need to write that page copy first. Add *both* tasks on the calendar, listing the writing task before the email marketing task.

6. Create an actual appointment for each task, estimating how long it will take to finish that task. If writing your sales page needs four hours of your personal time, create a task from 9:00 a.m. to 1:00 p.m. called "Write Sales Page Copy."

7. If you're unsure how long a task will take, use an educated guess and double it – *eight* hours to write your sales page. Humans are notoriously bad at estimating

how long a task will take, so by doubling your estimate, you allow some wiggle room.

8. Make sure you haven't added too many tasks in one day or one week. Super-productivity doesn't mean overburdening yourself or your team. Be practical about how much can be accomplished in day/week.

9. Remember to give yourself Murphy's Law Time – blank places on your calendar to use in case things don't go as planned. Murphy's Law says what can go wrong, will go wrong. Without getting cynical, we must accept that things don't always go according to plan – so plan for this Murphy's Law Time, add an extra day here and there, and you'll reduce your stress immeasurably.

10. Daily, look at the list of tasks you want to accomplish by the end of the week. This keeps you focused and on track with your projects and action plans.

Sometimes you only need a 15 minute "appointment" to complete a task. Other tasks might take longer. But creating an *all-day* task appointment just trips your amygdala switch. Instead, break down that full-day task appointment into its component parts.

For instance, as I'm finishing this One Action Now book, I've marked all day Wednesday, Thursday, and Friday for writing and editing. But within those full days, I have smaller tasks:

- Write the chapter on procrastination (2 hours).
- Edit the Gantt Chart example and insert it as an image in the book (1 hour).
- Find a book cover graphic designer (6 hours) Whoops,

too big of a task! I divided it into: Sign up for Upwork (15 minutes), review existing book cover designers on Upwork (1 hour), write a project request for Upwork (1.5 hours), post the project request on the Upwork website (15 minutes), ask colleagues if they know anyone who can do this type of work (30 minutes), etc.

By chunking my work down into small tasks, I'll have accomplished a huge amount by the end of the week – and my amygdala says, "I can do that!" without any resistance.

As I said earlier, I use Monday mornings to review my calendar, and all my open projects and tasks. I check to see if my calendar is still functional and reasonable, or if tasks need to be re-arranged. Emergencies do crop up, and tasks take more or less time than you originally planned. These frequent reviews provide a space to rethink and edit your calendar and your action plans.

Consider a Minimal Viable Project

Have you decided that your project is too big? When people start their project planning, they focus on massive, important projects like:

- I want to host a five-day retreat for my executives.
- I will launch my new product worldwide in two months.

It's not that these projects aren't doable – they are. But their scope is so huge that, should the project fail to give you the results you want, you've wasted time and money. If you're going for super-productivity, you can't afford to waste time. You need more certainty that you're going down the right path before you give it your all.

How can you test the waters to discover if a massive project is worth the time? There's a concept called a minimal viable product or a minimal viable project. It's a reduced project that's in alignment with the larger goals, but on a smaller scale. Most important, it can reveal if the full project is worthwhile with far less expenditure of time, money, and resources.

I'll give you a perfect example: I had an opportunity to write a book, and I wanted to create a *big* signature system and a *big* business model around the book. When I was planning it all out, I ended up creating four huge mind maps and a project that spanned three years.

Once it got that big, I began to think, "That's *too* big." Suddenly, the fear factor emerged and I was worried about how I would find the time and energy to get it all done. I didn't want to work two or three years to launch a new product, only to have it flop.

So, I asked myself which projects I could do first – ones that I'm competent at completing, and ones where I can easily get the help and resources I need. I discovered that there were two *smaller* projects I could work on that would help me discover if this big project was viable:

- I could update my research on how to write non-fiction book proposals. The last time I wrote a book proposal was over 10 years ago, so it was time to brush up on the process. If I felt that this process would be (relatively)

easy to do, it would signal that writing a book was a
reasonable goal.

- I could write a small e-book on the topic, perhaps 25
  pages, to see how my audience reacted. Not 200 or 300
  pages, just 25. Because I had written small e-books
  before, I felt competent enough to achieve this.

Doing these two projects helped break the logjam. I discovered
that, yes, I could write a book proposal based on the latest
publishing industry standards, so I was assured that part of the
larger project would be successful. Then I offered the 25-page e-
book to my audience and they bought it in droves. Now I knew my
audience was interested in the topic and I could safely assume
they'd be interested in my longer book, too. (Of course, there's
more to market research than testing the waters with a simple e-
book, but it's a good place to start.)

When you're working on a massive project and you're wondering
whether you should invest the resources to complete it, ask
yourself:

- Which one or two preliminary projects will help me
  recognize if this is the right bigger project?
- Is there a very small version of the larger project that I
  can create, to test the waters?
- Who can help me think through the pros and cons?
- Who can help me get this done quickly?

I was speaking with one of my clients this morning, and she told
me she had a lot of LinkedIn research to do, but it would take 20

hours. It was too big, and she didn't have time for this project. Through some creative brainstorming, she decided to hire her brother to do just two hours of LinkedIn research, essentially a mini-project to gather basic information. It's a very time-consuming and detail-oriented task, and he's great at that. He'll create a summary of his findings, and if two hours of research shows her that 20 hours of research is worth doing, she'll do it. (Better yet, she'll hire *him* to do it!)

Deal with the Feeling Overwhelmed

You might be feeling overwhelmed by all this project and task planning. Now that all these tasks are on your calendar, you're feeling pressure.

I've written an article that may help you. It's called *44 Ways to Deal with Overwhelm* (which you can find on the One Action Now Resources website: **www.oneactionnowbook.com/bookresources**). Here are some of my top tips:

First, understand why you're feeling overwhelmed. Many of my clients and students tell me they are feeling overwhelmed by running their own small business. It doesn't matter whether your business is brand new or 20 years old, there are many things to juggle as a business owner. You are not alone in feeling this way, and there are some very common reasons why we feel overwhelmed:

- Trying to be everything to everyone.
- Trying to focus on too many things at once.

- Being too optimistic about how much time it takes to do a task.
- Adding too many appointments and projects to your weekly calendar.
- Not saying "no" to energy-sucking people and projects.

Notice how all these things are a *choice* you made? Every time you make a choice to do too much, you choose to feel overwhelmed.

You are in control. You are in control of your calendar. You are in control of which projects are top priority. You are in control of your thoughts about your business. You're even in control about whether you answer a ringing phone or not.

The power is in your hands.

Here are some specific things you can do to help regain control:

1. **Say no without guilt.** Too often you try to please everyone and end up with too much on our plates. When you are feeling overwhelmed, look at the people and projects you've say Yes to that perhaps you should have said No to. Look at your to-do list and ask yourself if you can simply say No to any of the tasks. Remember, you are in control of your task list and your calendar. Only you can overbook yourself, so only you can say No to requests for your time. Learn specific ways to say No in the section entitled How to Say No later in the chapter.

2. **Clear your desk.** There is no better feeling than starting fresh and getting a complete handle on everything that needs to be done. By reviewing every

paper, every pile, every note, you consolidate and
prioritize.

3. **Do it.** Sometimes, a bare-knuckle commitment to
getting things done is necessary. That pesky colonoscopy
you've been putting off? Do it. That phone call to a
disgruntled vendor? Do it. That 3,000-word article?
Do it.

4. **Ditch it.** Some projects were never meant to be. Some
catalogs and magazines can be thrown away. Some videos
will never get watched. Get rid of them.

5. **Delegate it.** Ask for help. Look at all your tasks, and
for each one ask, "Am I the only person who can do this
task in the entire world?" Some tasks are your sole
providence; others can be delegated to a website
designer, graphic artist, administrative assistant, etc.

6. **Find it in 60 seconds or less.** Create a rule for
yourself that you can get your hands on anything in your
office in 60 seconds or less. When you put something
away, put it away in the most intuitive place you can
think of, so that it will be at your fingertips when you
need it. Find a home for every item in your office and
return it to its home after each use. Fall in love with your
filing cabinet.

7. **Celebrate.** When you get done with a large project,
don't automatically move to the next one. Find some
wonderful way to celebrate your achievement!

8. **Put on your CEO Hat.** What are priority tasks for
the ultimate success of your business? Sometimes what
seems like the right thing to do in the moment is exactly
the wrong thing to do for a positive future.

9. **Unsubscribe.** Do you receive too many email newsletters which you never read? I have a litmus test: Every quarter, I go through all the email newsletters I have received from a specific person. If I don't find at least one brilliant idea, one great tip, or one deep insight, I unsubscribe. By identifying why you subscribe to email newsletters or listen to podcasts, and using those values to judge whether it's delivering value to you, you'll easily be able to unsubscribe from those which no longer meet your needs.

10. **Perfectionism kills.** I know this because I tried to do every task perfectly and it nearly killed my business. Some tasks are critical for your success and need to be as good as they possibly can be. Other tasks are not so important and simply need to be done without a lot of glory or perfection.

11. **Action alleviates anxiety.** Pick one high-priority task on your To Do list and do it. Nothing relieves stress better than getting off your butt and getting into action. Don't fall in the trap of picking a low-priority task just because it is easy. Do the things that matter.

I want to give you as many tools in your back pocket as possible, so when you're feeling inundated you have an assortment of creative solutions. Every business owner feels swamped at one time or another. Of all the small business owners I've worked with, 70% report feeling overwhelmed *all the time*. Look at this list and pick two or three techniques that will give you something to try the next time you're feeling overwhelmed.

How to Stop Multitasking

It has repeatedly been proven that multitasking causes *twice the number of errors* than does focusing on one task at a time. Other studies show that people are *losing two hours a day to distractions and multitasking interruptions.*

To gain focus when working on your tasks, set aside time where you don't answer the phone or respond to emails or texts. Definitely carve out time when you don't visit social media sites or news websites (or visit cooking sites or watch puppy videos). Studies show that you can pay attention to something for about 10 to 17 minutes, then you need a mini-break.

Use the timer on your smartphone and set it for 17 minutes. Make an agreement with yourself that you will focus solely on one task for that 17 minutes, after which you can allow yourself a distraction break.

A distraction break, or a mini-break, is a short period of time, two or three minutes, when you do something else. Get a cup of coffee or just look out the window, something that clears your mind and distances you from the task at hand.

These *tune out* breaks are where you focus on something outside yourself. You might also enjoy *tune in* breaks where you might do some yoga, stretching, or meditation, and tune into what you're thinking and feeling in the moment. Tune out breaks are ways to distract your mind; tune in breaks center, calm and focus you again. Either is fine, but keep it to two or three minutes, then start another 17-minute cycle of focus.

Your brain needs time to focus – and it needs time to goof off. Your brain wants *both* conditions. You can train your brain to focus for longer and longer periods of time, but start first with 17 minutes, because you know your brain is naturally inclined to focus that long without a problem.

I hope this next sentence inspires you: I've trained my brain to the point where I can focus for over two hours at a time without a break. As I'm writing this very sentence, I've been working on this book, nonstop, for ninety minutes. And the next time you see me on Facebook, you can bet I'm on a tune out break.

It is possible to increase your focus; it just takes some practice.

Are You Pavlov's Dog?

When you are working on your projects, your built-in triggers cause reactions and distractions. But you can tame those triggers once you understand them.

Scientists always want to figure out why we do things. In one study, they examined what triggers us. They started with a dog: every time they rang a bell the dog got food. After a while he associated the bell with food. The bell became a trigger.

Then they started ringing the bell and *not* giving him food. Because the bell was a trigger, he would still salivate as if he was going to get food when he heard the bell. For him the bell meant food, and there was no way to disconnect the bell from his physical reaction to it, even when the reward was no longer given. I have the exact same reaction when driving past my favorite chocolate shop.

In your mind, does the email or text bell mean you must react instantly? Our bodies are conditioned to release stress hormones when we hear the notification sound from our devices. Instantly your brain prompts you, "Do something! Take action!" It's certainly more than mere habit: we are psychologically and biochemically conditioned to respond once we associate reward with checking email or Facebook.

I have watched people at a business lunch where we're supposed to be having a deep conversation. Their smartphone will ring or beep, and they instantly grab it and look at it, *even if they know they're not going to respond*. They can't stop themselves.

Do you want a device or a piece of software to have that kind of control over your mind?

What if you decided to turn it off when you don't want to be disturbed? If you recognize you're trained like Pavlov's dog to respond to the bell, turn off the bell for an hour or two. Yes, you may have withdrawal symptoms for a while, but they'll go away. When I'm with a client or teaching a class, I turn off my phone and exit from email and social media sites. When I'm at lunch with friends or colleagues, I don't turn on my phone.

Imagine the freedom you'll feel when the bells don't control you anymore. What would you do with that extra time and the feeling of focus, clarity, and peace?

How to Say No

Drawing up a brilliant 90-Day Action Plan can be wasted effort if you lack this important talent: the skill to say No.

Would you babysit my pet tarantula next week? No.

Is it okay if I bring my 15 cousins to your birthday party? No.

Can we extend our contract for six months but not increase the price? No.

Sometimes saying no is easy; at other times it's tricky and you're not sure how to word it diplomatically. Without the right words, you sometimes say yes when you don't mean it, causing stress, frustration, and bad feelings. To stay dedicated to getting your projects completed, you can't be at the beck and call of everyone who wants your time or attention. So how can you say no in the best way possible?

Here are some suggestions. While these are business-related, you can modify them for personal use as well.

When No Means No

- There's the always useful, plain old fashioned "No." Without preamble, without excuses, without guilt.
- I can't take on your project at this time.
- I'm not accepting any new clients.
- I'm not comfortable doing what you're asking.
- I'm not willing to do what you're asking (note the distinction between the words *comfortable* versus *willing*).
- I'm not the right person for the job.
- I have other commitments that prevent me from doing this.

- We have a policy in our business that we don't do that.
- My schedule is already busy and I'm committed to work/life balance.
- Right now, my priority is _____ (fill in the blank) and I'm declining everything else.
- I'm can't/won't take on that type of responsibility.
- Our original agreement was for _____; I'm not willing to change that agreement mid-stream.
- I have an appointment that I can't reschedule.
- I want to spend more time doing _____ .
- I don't enjoy that work.
- My decision is final.

When No Means I can't do _____, but I can offer _____ instead

- I'm not comfortable doing _____, but I'm available to do _____ within certain parameters.
- I'm not really qualified to do this work, but I can recommend an excellent person who might help you.
- I'd rather work on _____.
- I'd rather do it this way rather than the way you are suggesting.
- I can't do this myself, but I can ask my assistant to do it for you, if it takes only 30 minutes like you promised.
- That's too little money for this type of work. How about $500?

When No Means I can't do it now, but I can do it later

- I'm not accepting any new clients until September.
- Can we schedule this for next week instead?
- I'm booked solid for April.
- This Wednesday is bad for me.
- I don't work on Fridays.
- I need to leave work by 5:00 p.m.
- I can't work on it this week but I'll add it in my calendar for next week.

10 Tips for Managing Information Overload

Do you ever have that disturbing feeling that trying to squeeze one more piece of new information into your brain will render you senseless?

Information overload causes stress and a loss of productivity. You're so busy gathering information that you never seem to implement all these great ideas. It's frustrating to have a big, juicy list of ideas and stall when it comes to implementation. Worse, you can't seem to put your finger on the important information that you've gathered, which delays action-taking.

Here's even more bad news: when you absorb too much information, according to a Temple University study, you begin to make more errors and make more bad decisions. Can your business really afford that lack of clear thinking? (Don't even get me started about how a hyper-connected lifestyle is bad for your physical and emotional health.)

Here are 10 tips for managing information overload so you regain control of your brain, your time, and your tasks:

1. **Remember the most important rule: YOU are in charge.** *You* are in charge of your action plan and calendar. *You* are in charge of how much information you're willing to receive each day. Don't set yourself up for information overload by taking multiple classes simultaneously, or reading more than one book at a time, without setting up assimilation time to ponder how this information applies to your specific business goals and challenges. You need time to pause, reflect, and plan based on the new ideas coming in. Be selective with those new ideas and base all your decisions on achieving your goals while mirroring your values.

2. **Get things out of your head and onto paper.** When you take in reams of information, your brain naturally tries to process it, make connections, and apply it to your business life. When you attempt to keep all that thinking inside your head, you feel muddled, anxious, and confused. Do a brain dump and write down your ideas, even in a quick list format. This will clear your head and give you space to consolidate your thinking.

3. **Review the most recent class you've attended or the most recent book you've read and create a Top Three Action Items list.** Don't create a massive to-do list of every great idea from the class or book. Instead, choose the top three things which you can act on within a month, and add *only* those three things on your task list. Once they're done, you can

always go back and choose three more. The point is two-fold: start implementing what you've learned and do it in such a way that you don't overload yourself.

4. **Use tools like Evernote to have a central location for storing information.** As important as storing information is, *retrieving* it easily is even more important. That's why I moved from paper notebooks to a software app called Evernote for storing notes when taking classes, reading books, or perusing articles. Evernote allows you to tag each note with keywords and sort them into "notebooks." Notes are completely searchable, so you can have all the information and ideas you've accumulated at your fingertips. If you need to share this information with your team or vendor, look for an online shareable notetaking solution that synchronizes everyone's notes.

5. **Practice OMD: Off My Desk.** I have a bad habit of collecting thoughts on bits of paper, which form massive piles on my desk. Once a week, I have an OMD hour... every bit of paper gets looked at and acted upon, and the idea goes into Evernote or onto my action plan. The paper gets tossed, clearing space on my desk and in my brain.

6. **Decide to make a decision.** It sounds silly, right? But if ideas and information are running around in your head, and you don't decide to either act on them or let them go, you sabotage yourself in a perpetual state of overload. Stop doing that to yourself! Instead, tell yourself, "Today I will make a decision," and then do it. You'll immediately feel better.

7. **Stop saying, "I'm too distracted to focus."**
Choosing to focus on one goal or one task is a conscious
and strategic decision you make. You are perfectly
capable of focusing and getting things done, but you've
got to train yourself to do it. It takes practice, as does
reminding yourself that you are *choosing* to narrow your
focus instead of allowing yourself to get sidetracked. If
you want to be successful, you must do what successful
people do: focus. Focus is a decision. Focus is a skill you
can learn and enhance. Negative self-talk will only weigh
you down.

8. **When you are drowning in information, stop
piling on more.** It's okay to stop watching the evening
news. It's okay to stop reading articles or checking social
media sites several times a day. Each time you interact
with an information delivery system, guess what? More
information is shoved in your face. By taking a vacation –
even a short one – from information delivery systems,
you get immediate relief.

9. **Prioritize the information you allow into your
brain.** Let's say for a moment you're on LinkedIn and
you see a post with an interesting article. STOP RIGHT
THERE. Ask yourself: Is this article merely interesting
or is it really, truly important? Do I have time to read
interesting-but-not-important information right now?
How will this article help me achieve my overall goals?
By making choices about what to pay attention to, you
can escape information overload. And when you are
ready to read about a certain subject, that subject is just a
Google search away. Or choose a time each week when

you'll grab a cup of coffee and read several articles on LinkedIn all at once.

10. **Do you have competing goals? Work on one at a time.** For instance, today I wanted to accomplish three things: write a blog post, create my class schedule for the next nine months, and design a class agenda for a new program. All these tasks are exciting, and all need to get done – and all require research and paying attention to incoming information. But only one of the three had a deadline: the blog post is due tomorrow. So, I put the other tasks on the back burner and focused solely on researching and writing the blog post. Be willing to let go of some incoming information, even *exciting* information, so you can focus on your priorities.

Institute Quiet Time

Are you getting everything done on your 90-Day Action Plan? No? Join the crowd.

More and more professionals are complaining that email, phone calls, social media, and their beeping buzzing smart phones are constantly causing interruptions, increasing stress, and reducing productivity.

These constant interruptions are costing you. And if your team suffers from this, it's costing you their time and attention, too.

The Solution

Many large corporations like Intel, IBM, and Deloitte & Touche are instituting something called *quiet time*: a block of time in which you cannot send or read emails, and may not make or receive phone calls (unless they are related to the specific project you're working on). This concept of quiet time is so desirable that France established a law in 2017 which requires businesses with 50 or more employees to honor worker's "right to disconnect" at night and on the weekends to protect private time. If they can do it, you can do it, too!

I did a test last year and instituted quiet time in my work life:

- Core productivity times were 9:00 a.m. - 2:30 p.m. All private client calls, mastermind group meetings, classes, and project work were done during these hours. No emails, no extra phone calls, no long lunches.
- Every Friday was "class design and book writing day." No client or prospect appointments, no emails from 9:00 - 2:30, no phone calls at all.
- Action planning was handled first thing each morning. That way, I knew the focus of my day.
- Emails were handled twice a day - at 8:00 a.m. and 2:30 p.m. Phone calls were returned after 2:30 p.m. (which works well because of the time zone differences between the East and West coasts).
- When I seriously needed deep focus to work on a project, I brought my laptop to the lake, park, or library, taking my work to a quiet environment without possible

distractions. (I particularly like the lake because there's no Wi-Fi there. When I have no temptations, more work gets done.)

- No work *at all* in the evenings and weekends unless there's a looming deadline. This allowed a true disconnection and mental rest to happen, above and beyond quiet time during my work day.

The Results of My Quiet Time Test

So how did my quiet time test do? Was I any more productive or happy? In a 12-month period, I designed and launched *three* new classes (including a nine-week class which was a whopper to design), wrote *one* new book, designed *two* new websites, and overall had a more joyful and satisfied lifestyle and work environment. And my income went up 40%. Awesome!

Lest you think that you will be less productive if you institute quiet time in your business, think again. Having fixed times each day for email and phone calls increases your productivity, reducing the amount of time you spend on these tasks. I found I could get through 30 to 40 emails in a solid, planned hour, which would have consumed two hours if I had answered them in a scattered fashion throughout the day.

If you are frustrated because you're not accomplishing your projects and tasks, you need to schedule quiet time into each day. You'll be happier and feel more fulfilled by your work if you do, and best of all, you'll complete those visionary projects you've been dreaming of finishing!

For me, I continue to use quiet time as a daily practice.

Set Your Core Productivity Time

When are your core productivity times during the day or during the week?

I'm bright as a button on Mondays through Thursdays, but I'm less energetic on Fridays. I can get a huge amount of work done until about 3:00 in the afternoon and then my mental ability dwindles rapidly. After dinner, I get a second burst of energy from around 7:00 to 8:00 p.m. and then I'm done for the day.

Instead of judging yourself and assuming you "should" be productive 24/7, honestly ask yourself if there are certain times of the day, or certain days of the week, which you consider your core productivity time. Are there times when your mind is at its best?

Many business owners tell me that Saturday morning is their core productivity time. Their kids are off at soccer and the house is quiet (and they know it will stay quiet for hours). They're away from the office and they don't feel compelled on Saturday mornings to check business email. They can pour all their energy into an important project during that time. If your core productivity time is not during "normal working hours," that's okay, if it works for you. After all, what's the point of being self-employed if you must punch a 9-to-5 time clock?

It's all about getting the right task done at the right time – the times in your week when you're truly at your peak.

14

JUGGLING IT ALL

Wouldn't it be nice if you only had one project to work on? Reality dictates that you'll have multiple projects going at the same time, so keeping organized across all projects is a key skill. Here are some tips to help you be productive.

Master Project List

I like to have one central place where I can see a snapshot of all my projects and the next few tasks in each one. While it's important to have one action plan per project with tasks and deadlines clearly labelled, it's equally important to have a master calendar of *all* projects that are occurring simultaneously. This type of dashboard ensures you keep your fingers on the pulse of your business.

There are plenty of software tools that can help you with project management. Whichever one you choose, make sure there is a dashboard feature that shows you the status at a glance. You'll want one that allows you to easily move tasks and projects around. If you are sharing the project with your team or vendors, an online project management tools allows centralized updating and for you to see everything in one place on your dashboard.

I like to keep my personal action plan dashboard as a word processing document for the coming week. Each evening before I leave work, I edit the document, deleting the tasks I got done, and adding anything new that must be completed that week. It's a place to pause each day and think about what's important. I print it out and leave it on my desk so it's the first thing I see in the morning. This tactile approach works well for people who need to interact with their task list daily so it stays fresh in their minds.

Project Binders and Electronic Folders

Disorganization is the biggest killer of productivity. Where will you keep all your information and notes about your project so you can get your hands on anything in 60 seconds or less?

I keep my projects physically organized with a three-part filing system:

- All my physical project materials are in a binder or multi-pocket folder.
- For that same project, there's a digital folder on my hard drive.
- For notes and ideas about the project, I create an Evernote "notebook" to hold individual notes.

All three are named the same thing so it's easy to find what I'm looking for, whether it's electronic or on paper.

The binder holds my hand-drawn mind maps and blank paper for brainstorming, as well as any articles I've torn from print magazines. Smarter idea: scan those print articles, paper notes, mind maps and book pages, and store them electronically. The nice thing about the physical binder and the electronic folder on my hard drive is that they're portable. I grab the binder and my laptop, and I can work offsite when I want quiet time.

I use Evernote to keep my ideas organized. Evernote is a software app for taking notes and capturing thoughts. It's also a place to store project research, website links, images, or PDFs. It allows you to keep all your notes and ideas in one place. You can create a notebook for each of your topics or projects, and you can search across all notebooks for keywords.

As an example, I have a "marketing" notebook on Evernote where all the notes reside. If I read a website page or blog post on marketing and want to capture the information, the link URL goes into a note in Evernote. If I have some ideas about marketing for a specific product or service I'm launching, like a mastermind group, those go in a "mastermind group marketing" note. I can get as granular with the notebook levels as suits my needs. Here's an example of what my Marketing and Selling Notebook looks like in Evernote:

Because I can search across all notebooks and notes, if I search for "marketing" the note will pop up, and if I search for "mastermind groups" the same note will pop up. I don't have to remember where I put each note, I simply search for it and it appears.

Here's what I love about Evernote: if you're like me, you probably have more than one device you work on. I have my office computer – it has a huge screen that's great for writing and for researching on the internet. I also have my laptop, tablet, and a smartphone. I can record any idea that comes to me using any device, because Evernote synchronizes over the internet to all your devices. I write a note on my laptop, and when I open my smartphone, the same note appears. You'll never be without all your notes and ideas. There are other note-taking tools you can use, so find the one that works best for your needs.

One final tip: *do not* print out pages from the internet and place them in a folder. Instead, save a tree, and print the page to a PDF, then add that PDF in your project folder on your hard drive (or add it in Evernote). Most computers will allow you to print to PDF. Now all your research information is in one place, easy to find and easy to organize. And because it's digitized, you can search for keywords across all those PDFs, something you can't do easily with paper articles tucked in a filing folder.

EPILOGUE: THE BREATH-TAKING RESULTS

Naturally, this book has a happy ending. I created a more efficient business, made wiser decisions, and completed more projects on time and on budget. Some years my profits increased by 40%. We've launched major year-long signature education and mastermind group programs for our clients – what I thought was a fanciful pipe dream became a reality. I finished writing One Action Now.

Yes, those things happened – but here's some of the *unexpected* results:

- Because I got a handle on my original business, I was able to open a second business and run them both simultaneously. That's a theme throughout my career and today I continue to grow two businesses at the same time.

- When I got married, I decided that I'd rather spend my weekends with my new husband rather than photographing someone else's wedding. So, I sold my photography business. The biggest selling point? I had a *system* for running that business that the buyer found highly attractive.
- I can take vacations away from the business without worrying it will crumble in my absence. Occasionally I take an impromptu day off and enjoy the mountains where I live or have lunch with my sister.
- So much is streamlined and automated that I can devote huge chunks of time to super-important, long-term projects. The first and last weeks of the month are for clients and students, and I use the two middle weeks for writing books, designing classes, or whatever else is crucial for my business growth.
- My clients get the respectful, caring attention they deserve and many become close friends and business allies.

Eve and Tom are flourishing, too. Today, Eve has three studio locations with office managers in each one, and ten or more yoga classes happening every day. She's taught the One Action Now system to her staff and they run the studios seamlessly. Tom created a series of powerful educational videos about copywriting, and attracted a large fan base who wanted to attend his classes, too. He built a strong brand and scaled his business. He's thinking about whether he can retire early. He tells me he uses One Action Now every single day.

YOU DID IT!

Congratulations! You've now walked through the entire One Action Now system. You:

- Determined what's most important to you and selected goals that will support your values.
- Selected the right projects which will help you achieve your goals.
- Chose one project and broke it down into tasks.
- Identified which resources you'll need to tackle those tasks.
- Scheduled the tasks so that they are achievable: a true action plan.
- Learned new ways to keep focused, managing your time and attention.

These pieces make action planning tick and keep you productive.

Look over all these ideas and incorporate the ones that work for you. You'll be happy with how much you get done!

By including smart planning into every project, you're learning to master it and make it your own. Once you've mastered it – share it with your friends, colleagues, and clients so they can be successful, too.

I believe in you. I believe you are capable of learning what you need to learn to have a successful business. I believe you will find time in your day for all that needs to get done if you focus on taking *one action now*. I believe your dream is so important that you'll move mountains to get it – and I believe you *can* move mountains, with focus, perseverance, and strength...and a smart, savvy action plan.

FREE RESOURCES FOR YOU

It can be difficult to write on the pages of a printed paperback book, and for e-book readers it's impossible to use the worksheets in any meaningful way.

I've created a One Action Now Journal for you, which contains all the worksheets found in this book, plus some additional exercises and worksheets to move you forward:

- I Did It worksheet
- What's Most Important worksheet
- Goal Setting worksheet
- Project Wish List worksheet
- Goals Versus Projects worksheet
- Task List worksheet
- Tools, Knowledge and Resources worksheet
- Project Cost worksheet

- 90-Day Action Plan worksheet
- Design Your Perfect Week exercise
- Annual Values Planning exercise
- Understanding the Motivation Volcano
- Take the Leap and Grow Your Business Self-assessment

The One Action Now Journal is in PDF format. That way, you can either print a paper copy to write in, or fill in the blanks in the PDF itself.

In addition, there is an amazing array of resources available online. I collected "the best of the best" in one place for you on the Resources website. These include all my personally researched and curated video tutorials, articles, and websites. I've also include links to all the software and tools mentioned in One Action Now.

To access all these free resources, sign up here:

www.oneactionnowbook.com/bookresources

ABOUT KARYN GREENSTREET

Karyn Greenstreet is an internationally-known small business consultant, speaker, and mastermind group expert. She has owned five businesses over the past 30 years, and is the founder of Passion For Business and The Success Alliance.

She has taught business development topics to over 280,000 participants worldwide, sharing her passion about business growth and reaching your full potential as an owner. She helps seasoned business owners expand reach and revenue, get a clear vision of their scalable business model, and design proven strategies to create business and marketing efficiencies.

Deep-dive into your own action planning process at a One Action Now virtual workshop, and learn how to apply the One Action Now system to your business: www.OneActionNow.com

Let's connect!

FACEBOOK: www.facebook.com/KarynGreenstreet

LINKEDIN: www.linkedin.com/in/karyngreenstreet/

14821131R00112

Made in the USA
San Bernardino, CA
15 December 2018